First World War
and Army of Occupation
War Diary
France, Belgium and Germany

2 DIVISION
Divisional Troops
Royal Army Veterinary Corps
3 Mobile Veterinary Section
4 August 1914 - 28 October 1919

WO95/1340/1

The Naval & Military Press Ltd
www.nmarchive.com
Published in association with The National Archives

Published by

The Naval & Military Press Ltd

Unit 10 Ridgewood Industrial Park,

Uckfield, East Sussex,

TN22 5QE England

Tel: +44 (0) 1825 749494

www.naval-military-press.com

www.nmarchive.com

This diary has been reprinted in facsimile from the original. Any imperfections are inevitably reproduced and the quality may fall short of modern type and cartographic standards.

© Crown Copyright
Images reproduced by permission of The National Archives, London, England, 2015.

Contents

Document type	Place/Title	Date From	Date To
Heading	1340/1 1914 Aug-1919 Oct 3 Mobile Vet Sec		
Heading	2nd. Division War Diaries No. 3 Veterinary Mobile Section August To December 1914		
Heading	2nd. Div L. 1C' No. 3 Vety Mobile Section Volume I Aug 1914		
War Diary	Aldershot	04/08/1914	18/08/1914
War Diary	Boulogne	19/08/1914	21/08/1914
War Diary	Vaux	22/08/1914	22/08/1914
War Diary	Boue	22/08/1914	23/08/1914
War Diary	Landrecies	23/08/1914	24/08/1914
War Diary	Mennevret	25/08/1914	25/08/1914
War Diary	Le Groise	25/08/1914	25/08/1914
War Diary	Etreux	25/08/1914	26/08/1914
War Diary	St. Quentin	26/08/1914	26/08/1914
War Diary	Ham	26/08/1914	27/08/1914
War Diary	Noyon	27/08/1914	28/08/1914
War Diary	Barencourt	29/08/1914	29/08/1914
War Diary	Camelin	29/08/1914	29/08/1914
War Diary	Pierremand	29/08/1914	30/08/1914
War Diary	Soissons	30/08/1914	31/08/1914
War Diary	Laversine	31/08/1914	31/08/1914
Heading	War Diary Of Captain W.H. Taylor A.V.C. 6C No. 3 Mobile Veterinary Section 1.9.14 To 30.9.14		
War Diary	Bouriome	01/09/1914	01/09/1914
War Diary	Rosay	02/09/1914	13/09/1914
War Diary	Sime	14/09/1914	14/09/1914
War Diary	Dhuizel	15/09/1914	19/09/1914
War Diary	Mont-Notre Dame	20/09/1914	20/09/1914
War Diary	Fere-En-Tardenois	21/09/1914	25/09/1914
War Diary	Dhuizel	26/09/1914	26/09/1914
War Diary	Braine	27/09/1914	28/09/1914
War Diary	Dhuizel	29/09/1914	30/09/1914
Heading	No. 3 Mobile Vety Section Volume III October 1914		
War Diary	Dhuizel	01/10/1914	09/10/1914
War Diary	Braine	09/10/1914	09/10/1914
War Diary	Dhuizel	10/10/1914	15/10/1914
War Diary	St. Omer	16/10/1914	17/10/1914
War Diary	Hazebrouck	17/10/1914	21/10/1914
War Diary	Ypres	22/10/1914	31/10/1914
Heading	II Div. 3 Mobile Section A.V.C. Vol IV Nov 1914		
War Diary	Vlamertinghe	01/11/1914	18/11/1914
War Diary	Poperinghe	18/11/1914	18/11/1914
War Diary	Hazebrouck	18/11/1914	30/11/1914
Heading	2nd. Division No. 3 Mobile Section A.V.C. Vol V 1-31.12.14		
War Diary	Caestre	01/12/1914	23/12/1914
War Diary	Bethune	24/12/1914	26/12/1914
War Diary	Locon	27/12/1914	31/12/1914
Heading	2nd. Division War Diaries No. 3 Mobile Vety Section From 1st. January To 30th. November 1915		

Heading	2nd. Division No. 3 Mobile Vety Section Vol VI Jan 1915		
War Diary	Locon	01/01/1915	31/01/1915
Heading	2nd. Division No. 3 Mobile Vety Section Vol VII Feb 1915		
War Diary	Locon	01/02/1915	04/02/1915
War Diary	Bethune	05/02/1915	28/02/1915
Heading	2nd. Division No. 3 Mobile Vety Section Vol VIII 1-31.3.15		
War Diary	Bethune	01/03/1915	31/03/1915
Heading	2nd. Division No. 3 Mobile Vety Section Vol IX 1-30.4.15		
War Diary	Bethune	01/04/1915	30/04/1915
Heading	2nd. Division No. 3 Mobile Vety Section Vol X 1-31.5.15		
War Diary	Bethune	01/05/1915	12/05/1915
War Diary	Locon	13/05/1915	28/05/1915
War Diary	Ames	29/05/1915	31/05/1915
Heading	2nd. Division No. 3 Mobile Vety Section Vol XI 1-30.6.15		
War Diary	Ames	01/06/1915	09/06/1915
War Diary	Hesdigneul	10/06/1915	28/06/1915
War Diary	Bethune	29/06/1915	30/06/1915
Heading	2nd. Division No. 3 Mobile Vety Section Vol XII July August & Sept 15		
War Diary	Bethune	01/07/1915	02/10/1915
Heading	2nd. Division 3rd. Mobile Vety Section Oct-15 Vol XII		
War Diary	In The Field	01/10/1915	01/10/1915
War Diary	At Poperinghe	02/10/1915	23/10/1915
War Diary	St. Trenvande	24/10/1915	31/10/1915
Heading	2nd. Division No. 3 Mob Vet Sec Oct To Nov Vol XIV		
War Diary		03/10/1915	30/11/1915
Heading	2nd. Division Divl. Troops No. 3 Mobile Veterinary Sec Dec 1915-Dec 1916		
Heading	War Diary Of No. 3 M.V.S. 2nd. Div. From Dec 1st. 1915 To Apl 30th. 1916		
War Diary	Bethune	01/12/1915	29/12/1915
War Diary	Busnes	30/12/1915	17/01/1916
War Diary	Bethune	18/01/1916	23/02/1916
War Diary	Busnes	24/02/1916	27/02/1916
War Diary	Bethune	28/02/1916	29/02/1916
War Diary	Barlin	01/03/1916	21/03/1916
War Diary	Bruay	22/03/1916	18/04/1916
War Diary	Barlin	19/04/1916	30/04/1916
Heading	War Diary Of No. 3 Mobile Veterinary Section 2nd. Div. From May 1st-16 To May 31st.-16		
War Diary	Barlin	01/05/1916	16/05/1916
War Diary	Bruay	17/05/1916	27/05/1916
War Diary	Fresnicourt	28/05/1916	31/05/1916
Heading	War Diary Of No. 3 M.V.S. 2nd. Div. From June 1st-16 To June 30th.-16 Vol 21		
War Diary	Fresnicourt	01/06/1916	30/06/1916
Heading	No. 3 Mob Vet Section Vol 22		
Heading	War Diary Of No. 3 M.V.S. From July 1st.-16 To July 31st.-16		
War Diary	Fresnicourt	01/07/1916	18/07/1916

War Diary	Dieval	19/07/1916	21/07/1916
War Diary	Saleux	21/07/1916	21/07/1916
War Diary	Daours	22/07/1916	27/07/1916
War Diary	Bray	28/07/1916	31/07/1916
Heading	War Diary Of No. 3 M.V.S. From Aug 1st.-16 To Aug 31st.-16 (Vol 1)		
War Diary	Grovetown	01/08/1916	10/08/1916
War Diary	Daours	11/08/1916	11/08/1916
War Diary	Sailly Sur Somme	12/08/1916	12/08/1916
War Diary	St. Savoeur	13/08/1916	15/08/1916
War Diary	Vignacourt	16/08/1916	16/08/1916
War Diary	Bernacourt	17/08/1916	17/08/1916
War Diary	Bus Les Artois	18/08/1916	19/08/1916
War Diary	Couin	20/08/1916	31/08/1916
Heading	War Diary Of No. 3 M.V.S. From Sept 1st.-16 To Sept 30th.-16 Vol 24		
War Diary	Couin	01/09/1916	02/10/1916
War Diary	Vauchelles	03/10/1916	31/10/1916
Heading	War Diary Of No. 3 M.V.S. From Nov 1st.-16 To Nov 30th.-16		
War Diary	Bus Les Artois	01/11/1916	19/11/1916
War Diary	Doullens	20/11/1916	21/11/1916
War Diary	Bernaville	22/11/1916	23/11/1916
War Diary	Fransu	24/11/1916	25/11/1916
War Diary	Brailly	26/11/1916	26/11/1916
War Diary	Yvrench	27/11/1916	27/11/1916
War Diary	Neuville	28/11/1916	30/11/1916
Heading	War Diary Of No. 3 M.V.S. From Dec 1st. 1916 To Dec 31st. 1916 (Vol 1)		
War Diary	Neuville	01/12/1916	31/12/1916
Heading	2nd. Division Divl. Troops No. 3 Mobile Vety Section 1917 Jan-1918 Dec		
Heading	War Diary Of No. 3 M.V.S. From Jany 1st.-17 To Jany 31st.-17 (Vol 1)		
War Diary	Neuville	01/01/1917	09/01/1917
War Diary	Bernaville	10/01/1917	11/01/1917
War Diary	Marieux	12/01/1917	13/01/1917
War Diary	Bouzincourt	14/01/1917	31/01/1917
Heading	War Diary Of No. 3 M.V.S. From Feb 1st. 1917 To Feby 28th. 1917 (Vol 1)		
War Diary	Bouzincourt	01/02/1917	28/02/1917
Heading	War Diary Of No. 3 M.V.S. From March 1st. 1917 To March 31st. 1917 (Vol 1)		
War Diary	Bouzincourt	01/03/1917	24/03/1917
War Diary	Contay	25/03/1917	25/03/1917
War Diary	Beauval	26/03/1917	26/03/1917
War Diary	Bouquemaison	26/03/1917	27/03/1917
War Diary	Ramecourt	28/03/1917	29/03/1917
War Diary	Pernes	30/03/1917	31/03/1917
Heading	War Diary Of No. 3 Mobile Veterinary Section. From April 1st. 1917 To April 30th. 1917 (Vol I)		
War Diary	Pernes	01/04/1917	07/04/1917
War Diary	Monchy Breton	08/04/1917	09/04/1917
War Diary	Haute Avesnes	10/04/1917	14/04/1917
War Diary	Bray	15/04/1917	22/04/1917
War Diary	Ecoivres	23/04/1917	30/04/1917

Type	Location	From	To
Heading	War Diary Of No. 3 Of M.V.S. From May 1st. 1917 To May 31st. 1917 (Vol I)		
War Diary	Ecoivres	01/05/1917	31/05/1917
Heading	War Diary Of No. 3 M.V.S. From June 1st.-17 To June 30th.-17 (Vol I)		
War Diary	Ecoivres	01/06/1917	20/06/1917
War Diary	Bethune	21/06/1917	30/06/1917
Miscellaneous	A.O. Quarters 2nd. Div.	06/08/1917	06/08/1917
Heading	War Diary Of No. 3 M.V.S. From July 1st. 1917 To July 31st. 1917 (Vol 1)		
War Diary	Bethune	01/07/1917	31/07/1917
Heading	War Diary Of No. 3 M.V. Section From Aug 1st. 1917 To Aug 31st. 1917 (Vol 1)		
War Diary	Bethune	01/08/1917	31/08/1917
Heading	War Diary Of No. 3 M.V.S From Sept 1st. 1917 To Sept 30th. 1917 (Vol 1)		
War Diary	Bethune	01/09/1917	06/10/1917
War Diary	La Fontonille Farm	07/09/1917	31/10/1917
War Diary	Labouvriere	01/11/1917	05/11/1917
War Diary	Busnes	06/11/1917	06/11/1917
War Diary	Merville	07/11/1917	07/11/1917
War Diary	Eecke	08/11/1917	08/11/1917
War Diary	Herzule	09/11/1917	10/11/1917
War Diary	Wormhoudt	11/11/1917	24/11/1917
War Diary	Bapaume	25/11/1917	30/11/1917
Miscellaneous	D.A.G., G.H.Q., 3rd Echelon	14/01/1918	14/01/1918
War Diary	Bectriot Factory Etricourt	01/12/1917	31/01/1918
War Diary	Etricourt V2 Central	01/02/1918	28/02/1918
War Diary	Bectriot Factory Etricourt	01/03/1918	22/03/1918
War Diary	Beaulancourt	23/03/1918	23/03/1918
War Diary	Meaulte	24/03/1918	24/03/1918
War Diary	Vadencourt	25/03/1918	28/03/1918
War Diary	Doullens	29/03/1918	31/03/1918
War Diary	Fontencourt	01/04/1918	05/04/1918
War Diary	Doullens Frevent	07/04/1918	12/04/1918
War Diary	Couturville	13/04/1918	30/04/1918
Heading	War Diary No. 3 Mobile Veterinary Section For May 1918		
War Diary	Port Sueg	24/04/1918	24/04/1918
War Diary	Muascan	26/04/1918	21/05/1918
War Diary	Bavincourt	01/05/1918	07/06/1918
War Diary	Humbercamp	07/06/1918	28/08/1918
War Diary	Pommier	29/08/1918	02/09/1918
War Diary	Douchy	03/09/1918	03/09/1918
War Diary	Ervillers	04/09/1918	05/09/1918
War Diary	Mory	06/09/1918	30/09/1918
War Diary	Havrincourt	01/10/1918	03/10/1918
War Diary	Ribecourt	04/10/1918	08/10/1918
War Diary	Doignies	10/10/1918	13/10/1918
War Diary	Noyelles	14/10/1918	20/10/1918
War Diary	Igniel	21/10/1918	23/10/1918
War Diary	St. Hilaire	24/10/1918	05/11/1918
War Diary	Vertain	06/11/1918	10/11/1918
War Diary	Villers Pol	11/11/1918	18/11/1918
War Diary	Mecquegnies	19/11/1918	20/11/1918
War Diary	Maubeuge	21/11/1918	24/11/1918

War Diary	Haulchin	25/11/1918	25/11/1918
War Diary	Fontaine L'Eveque	26/11/1918	29/11/1918
War Diary	Sart Eustache	30/11/1918	04/12/1918
War Diary	Wepion	05/12/1918	05/12/1918
War Diary	Thon	06/12/1918	06/12/1918
War Diary	Huy	07/12/1918	07/12/1918
War Diary	Ouffet	08/12/1918	08/12/1918
War Diary	Camblain La Tour	09/12/1918	09/12/1918
War Diary	Vert Boisson	10/12/1918	11/12/1918
War Diary	Ster	12/12/1918	12/12/1918
War Diary	Lager Elsenborn	13/12/1918	13/12/1918
War Diary	Witzereth	14/12/1918	14/12/1918
War Diary	Winden	15/12/1918	19/12/1918
War Diary	Oberzier	20/12/1918	24/12/1918
War Diary	Bickesdorf	25/12/1918	31/12/1918
Heading	2 Div. Troops 3 Mob Vet Sect 1919 Jan To 1919 Oct		
War Diary	Berkesdorf	01/01/1919	07/04/1919
War Diary	Bettenhoven	08/04/1919	18/04/1919
War Diary	Hollenholz Farm	19/04/1919	30/04/1919
War Diary	Hohenholz Farm	01/05/1919	31/05/1919
War Diary	Hohenholz Farm	27/05/1919	12/07/1919
War Diary	Ohligs	13/07/1919	28/10/1919

1340/

1914 Aug - 1919 Oct

3 Mobile Vet. Sec

2nd/K Division

War Diaries

No 3 Vet'y Mobile Section

August. To December 1914

121/1084

L.T.C.

No 3. Vity turkh declin

Volume I

Confidential   Vol. 1

War Diary of O.C. No 3 Mobile Veterinary Section from 4.8.14 to 31.8.14

Army Form C. 2118.

WAR DIARY
or
INTELLIGENCE SUMMARY.
(Erase heading not required.)

Instructions regarding War Diaries and Intelligence Summaries are contained in F. S. Regs., Part II. and the Staff Manual respectively. Title pages will be prepared in manuscript.

Hour, Date, Place	Summary of Events and Information	Remarks and references to Appendices
6.40 PM. 4·8·14. ALDERSHOT.	Orders received to mobilize No 3. M.V.S.	
5·8·14 "	1st Day of mobilization. Medical inspection of serving soldiers.	
6·8·14 "	Took over billet, were at Army Veterinary School. Inspection of reservists. Barrack equipment to Quarmasters Medical inspection of reservists. Marking & issuing of equipment for reservists. Rifles not ready.	
7·8·14 "		
8·8·14 "	Rifles not ready. Personnel complete. Batmen posted from BRISTOL.	
9·8·14 "	Went to Central Remount Depot; Horses not ready. Notified that by 9·14 we can draw from thence.	
10·8·14 "	1st day of Mobilization. Harness drawn. Saddlery fitted. Mob. complete except for shoeing. Men inoculated.	
11·8·14 "	Shoeing completed. Entrained in marching order from 2.45 P.M. to 11 P.M.	
12·8·14 "	Entraining continued work. Entrained in marching order.	
13·8·14 "	Paid section.	"
14·8·14 "	Continue work.	

Army Form C. 2118.

WAR DIARY
or
INTELLIGENCE SUMMARY.
(Erase heading not required.)

Instructions regarding War Diaries and Intelligence Summaries are contained in F. S. Regs., Part II. and the Staff Manual respectively. Title pages will be prepared in manuscript.

Hour, Date, Place	Summary of Events and Information	Remarks and references to Appendices
15.8.14. ALDERSHOT.	Routine work.	
16.8.14	"	
17.8.14	"	
7.15am 18.8.14	Paraded in marching order.	
	Arrived at G. Sidney ALDERSHOT at 8 a.m.	
8.30 am	Left ALDERSHOT by train.	
10.30 am	Arrived at SOUTHAMPTON.	
10 PM	Left SOUTHAMPTON	
10.15 am 19.8.14 BOULOGNE	Arrived at BOULOGNE	
2.30 PM	Marched to Port Reuilli Camp. (Rest camp.)	
6 PM	Arrived at "	
10 am 20.8.14 "	Received verbal orders from Staff before we date of departure as follows :—	
	From No. 204. Platform No 2 11.15 am 21.8.14.	
	Advance party to be at station 12.15 PM on 21.8.14.	
	Main body " " " at 12.15 PM 17	
11 am 21.8.14 "	Left Rest Camp at 11am. Arrived at No 2 platform at 12.15 PM 17	
	Entrained at 1 PM.	
	Left No. 2 platform 1.45 PM	

Army Form C. 2118.

WAR DIARY
or
INTELLIGENCE SUMMARY.
(Erase heading not required.)

Instructions regarding War Diaries and Intelligence Summaries are contained in F. S. Regs., Part II. and the Staff Manual respectively. Title pages will be prepared in manuscript.

Hour, Date, Place	Summary of Events and Information	Remarks and references to Appendices
4.30 a.m. 22.8.14 VAUX	Arrival at GARE-DE-VAUX. Received orders at 5am from A.A. & QMG to proceed by road to BOVÉ & await further orders.	
8.45 a.m. 22.8.14 BOVÉ	Arrival at BOVÉ. Billeted men & available horses.	
23.8.14. 6.50 pm	Awaiting orders. Received telegram from commdn to proceed by road to LANDRECIES and report on arrival.	
7.30 pm		
11.20 pm LANDRECIES	Report arrival & reported at LANDRECIES until M.S. MV.S. A/Commander in AMIENS.	
24.8.14. 2.30 pm	Bivouacked at LANDRECIES. Handed telegram re Advanced Veterinary Hospital, opened at AMIENS dated 22.8.14	
1 pm	Received orders re collection of horses.	
2.45 pm	Proceeded to collect horses. Collected 2 horses from LE GROISE, ETREUX	
	" 6 " at MEMMEVRET.	
9.30 pm	Billeted with 1 A.C.G. at MEMMEVRET for the night.	

WAR DIARY
or
INTELLIGENCE SUMMARY.
(Erase heading not required.)

Army Form C. 2118.

Instructions regarding War Diaries and Intelligence Summaries are contained in F.S. Regs, Part II. and the Staff Manual respectively. Title pages will be prepared in manuscript.

Hour, Date, Place	Summary of Events and Information	Remarks and references to Appendices
25.8.14. 6 am HENNEVEUX	Sent 6 horses from HENNEVEUX by rail to AMIENS. Wired to Vet. AMIENS re details of horses & notified that section now at LANDRECIES. Collected 1 horse at LE GROISE & marched it to LANDRECIES.	
" 10 am	Received copy of Telegram from CAPT. HODGINS, moved from Vet. AMIENS in charge of mailcart.	
" LE GROISE 10 am	Marched to LANDRECIES Station & Trucked 5 horses to AMIENS.	
" 11 am	Marched the first to Vet. AMIENS, also that No. 3 Station was moving to ETREUX to day.	
" 1.15 am	arrived by road at ETREUX.	
ETREUX 4 PM	Marched to WASSIGNY to collect horses billeted. 6 horses & sent them from GUISE to ROUEN.	
6 am 26.8.14 "	Sent Lt. TOPHAM to collect 1 horse at BROUGIS and that left to the train at ST. QUENTIN.	
1 PM "		
4 PM 26.8.14 ST. QUENTIN	arrived from the train at ST. QUENTIN. Received orders left by CAPT. HODGINS for section to proceed to NOYON. Shells & cant remained at ST QUENTIN and abandoned, not taken on Mule lorry to NOYON.	
8 PM "	Met CAPT HODGINS en route to HAM and was told that section were to march with to "Dur. Ann. Col. to NOYON.	
11 PM HAM	Halted at HAM station for the night.	

(9 29 6) W 3332—1107 100,000 10/13 H W V Forms/C. 2118/10.

WAR DIARY or INTELLIGENCE SUMMARY

Army Form C. 2118.

Instructions regarding War Diaries and Intelligence Summaries are contained in F.S. Regs., Part II. and the Staff Manual respectively. Title pages will be prepared in manuscript.

(Erase heading not required.)

Hour, Date, Place		Summary of Events and Information	Remarks and references to Appendices
9 am 27.8.14	HAM	Staked round to NOYON. Left TOPHAM missing.	
1 p.m. "	NOYON	Arrived at NOYON. Wrote D.G. I.T.I. on purchase of cart to wheeled cart furnished by Commune. Received cheque for fr. 200 & orders from D.G.M.T. to join 2nd Div at 1st Wednesday.	
9 am 28.8.14	NOYON	Went to G. H.Q. 2/6 at NOYON & asked whereabouts of 2nd Div.	
10 am "	"	Left NOYON & marched in finister of CHAUNY to join 2nd Division. Collected 6 horses along the road. Billets for night at BARENCOURT.	
7.30 am 29.8.14	BARENCOURT	Went to stations BARENCOURT STATION & ROUEN & asked whereabouts of 2nd Div by telegram. No answer. Marched to CAMELIN & camped with 3mm Col. 3rd Div.	
12 Noon "	"		
2 p.m. "	CAMELIN	War, Bull. & Staff Officer that H. Q. 2nd Div was then at SERVAIS. SERVAIS.	
3 p.m. "		Marching towards SERVAIS.	

Army Form C. 2118.

WAR DIARY
or
INTELLIGENCE SUMMARY.
(Erase heading not required.)

Instructions regarding War Diaries and Intelligence Summaries are contained in F. S. Regs., Part II. and the Staff Manual respectively. Title pages will be prepared in manuscript.

Hour, Date, Place	Summary of Events and Information	Remarks and references to Appendices
6.30 p.m. 29.8.14. PERREMAND	Coupled for night with 2nd Div. Amm. Col. Reports arrived by messenger to A.D.V.S. 2nd Div. & orders for order.	
3 a.m. 30.8.14. "	Marched with column toward SOISSONS.	
3 p.m. " SOISSONS	Met A.D.V.S. at SOISSONS with Hd. Qs. 2nd Div. Received orders to go with them to 2nd Div. Bivouacked with Hd. Qrs. & town of SOISSONS.	
8 p.m. "	Received orders from A.D.V.S. to rejoin No 6 Field Ambulance and not moving. Collected 3 horses.	
11.5 a.m. 31.8.14. "	Marching towards LAVERSINE.	
6 p.m. " LAVERSINE	Arrived " 4 p.m. Rejoined No. 6 Field Ambulance & reported to A.D.V.S. that ambulance was not fighting.	
8 p.m. "	Detained 1 horse of 15 to M.T.C. (unwilling).	
9 p.m. "	Marching towards BOURSONNE.	

(9 29 6) W 3332—1107 100,000 10/13 H W V Forms/C. 2118/10.

AVD

M/Tm
121/1641

War Diary of

Captain W. H. Taylor A.V.C.
O.C. No 3 Mobile Veterinary Section

1.9.14 to 30.9.14

Vol. 2

War Diary of O.C. No 3 Mobile Veterinary Station from 1.9.14 to 30.9.14.
Officer W.H. Taylor AVC

Army Form C. 2118.

WAR DIARY
or
INTELLIGENCE SUMMARY.
(Erase heading not required.)

Hour, Date, Place	Summary of Events and Information	Remarks and references to Appendices
7.15 a.m. 1.9.14. Bonnerue	Arrived at Bonnerue 7.15 a.m. Left Bonnerue at 1 P.M. and marched to Roney and camped there for the night.	
2.9.14. Roney 6 a.m. 4.15. 11.30 a.m.	Marching J.W. to Roney. Arrived at Chaulefeld. (S.W.S. Meaux) Destroyed N.B. Horse belonging to 356 N.S.C. (Strata Lumalier) Arrived at Couloumiers.	
3.9.14. 4.9.14. 6.30 a.m. 5.30 P.M.	Received orders from A.D.V.S. to march with Hd. Qrs. 2 Divnop. Marched to Chateau Bilhertrain arriving about 12 Noon & infants marched to ADV 2 Marched to Faremier arriving about 9 P.M.	
5.9.14	Marched to Fontenay arriving about 3 P.M. Destroyed one horse "H" (Russer) Red injured fetlock Collectes A horses in route.	
6.9.14. 8.30 a.m. 8.30 P.M.	Left Fontenay Arrived at Rozoy (Pd 245 2nd Div.)	

War Diary of Captain W. D. Taylor, A.V.C. O.C. No. 3 M.V.S.

WAR DIARY
or
INTELLIGENCE SUMMARY.
(Erase heading not required.)

Army Form C. 2118.

Hour, Date, Place	Summary of Events and Information	Remarks and references to Appendices
7.9.14 11 a.m. 3. P.M.	Unit instructed to meet sick horses to Mobile Veterinary Section at Rozoy. Collected 82 Battery horse went to 2nd Division. Started & went in search for Vermand. Collected 14 horses en route. Bivouacked a the note, injuries severe.	
7. P.M.	Halted at a farm for night — about 6 made 1/f Rozoy. Watered & fed. Rode horse in.	
8.9.14 7 a.m.	Commenced march to Vermand with 95 horses. 6 unsuitable cases had to be destroyed before proceeding on march. Arrived at Vermand & returned 93 horses for Ahorned Base Vet Hospital.	
12 Noon		
9.9.14 2. 6 a.m.	Unit return march to rejoin 2nd Div. Sellite on.	
8 P.M.	Left at Rozoy. Arrived at Coulomiers.	

3/

War Diary of Lieut. W.J. Tupper A.V.C. O.C. No 3 M.V.S.

Army Form C. 2118.

WAR DIARY
or
INTELLIGENCE SUMMARY.
(Erase heading not required.)

Hour, Date, Place	Summary of Events and Information	Remarks and references to Appendices
9.9.14	Was informed by Depot & RE that Vet. Sec. 2nd Div. might be at Chatty-sur-Marne.	
6.30 PM	Arrived at La Ferté and camped for night. Ret. named horses shot at Lucken Rhys.	
9 PM	Sent message by Depot to to A.D.V.S. that No 3 Mobile Vet Sec. Section was at La Ferté & was proceeding to Vet. Sec. 2nd Div. tomorrow 10.9.14.	
10.9.14. 5 am	Commenced march to rejoin 2nd Div.	
10 P.M.	Reported to A.D.V.S. notified of action.	
11.9.14.	Marched with Vet. Sec. 26.15 Oulchy-le-Château. Drew forage for half pay months, & fuel rations. Weather very wet.	
12.9.14.	Marched to Glanville with Vet. Sec. Got rations my unit.	
13.9.14 6 PM	Received orders from A.D.V.S. to march with 2nd Div. Supply Train to Ptisie & joined 2nd Div. Supply train. Marched to	

War Diary of 1st Lieut. W. J. Taylor, A.V.C. B.E.F., M.V.S.

Army Form C. 2118.

WAR DIARY
or
INTELLIGENCE SUMMARY.
(Erase heading not required.)

Hour, Date, Place	Summary of Events and Information	Remarks and references to Appendices
14.9.14 11.30 a.m. Front	Marched towards Vieil Arcy & camped about 1 mile S.E. of that place in a Reserve area. Received orders from the A.D.V.S. to collect 3 horses belonging to the R.E. left at D'Huizel & wait for night to march on Braisne — Vieil Arcy road.	
15.9.14. 4.30 a.m. DHUIZEL	Marched to DHUIZEL with 2nd Div. Trains. ½ mile distant. Bivouaced at DHUIZEL. Weather very wet.	
16.9.14. "	Remained at DHUIZEL. Weather continues wet.	
17.9.14 DHUIZEL	Capt. Upham A.V.C. rejoins from Advanced Base &c(?) Armed with letter & 10 horses from 15th Armoured & one from Armoured Brigade adjut. says chestnut (Rumour?) not fit for but challenges from Army(?). Sent arrangt to A.D.V.S. reference removal of mules from to avail head. Weather very wet.	
19.9.14 "	Collecting more horses. Receipt and cycles from A.D.V.S. to contact with horses to Give - en - Tardenois.	

5 War Diary of 4th (London) M.A.V.C. (?) Army Form C. 2118.

WAR DIARY
or
INTELLIGENCE SUMMARY.
(Erase heading not required.)

Instructions regarding War Diaries and Intelligence Summaries are contained in F.S. Regs., Part II. and the Staff Manual respectively. Title pages will be prepared in manuscript.

Hour, Date, Place	Summary of Events and Information	Remarks and references to Appendices
19.9.14 DHUIZEL 2 PM	White Lta. 9/5 horses from 2nd Div. Horses for and heard.	
6 PM	Bivouac'd for night at Mont Notre Dame. Detached an horse of 15" Division (motive force)	
20.9.14 MONT-NOTRE-DAME 7.30 am	md Proceeding to meet heart.	
11.45 am	Detached 3 horses (mobile cases). Arrived at FERE-EN-TARDENOIS. Reported to D.D.V.S. Officer. No forage available. Learnt with such horses 1 mile S.E. of town. Sent party to station to await orders of R.T.O. Drew 2 units shel of from D.D.V.S. Officer.	
3.45 PM 21.9.14 FERE-EN-TARDENOIS 5.45 PM	Received note from R.T.O. that trucks would be available at 8.30 P.M. 9.3 horses entrained. 1/1 men & 15" horses proceeding to Remount Depot & 7 men & 1 Officer accompanied horses	

War Diary of Captain W.W. Faulkner AVC No. 3 M.V.I.

Army Form C. 2118.

WAR DIARY
or
INTELLIGENCE SUMMARY.
(Erase heading not required.)

Hour, Date, Place	Summary of Events and Information	Remarks and references to Appendices
6 PM. 21.9.14 FÈRE-EN-TARDENOIS	Sent horse cart with NCO's to G.H.Q. to G.E. Advanced Base Veterinary Hospital at Villeneuve	
6 PM	ST-GEORGES. Reported intending to move to D.D.V.S.	
7.30 am 22.9.14	Started to rejoin 2nd Div.	
7.45 am	Reported departure to D.D.V.S.	
1 PM	Had to return, horse shot at Mont-NOTRE-DAME.	
5 PM.	Arrived at DHUIZEL & joined with Train	
10 PM - 23.9.14 10 PM	Rode to Hill 26. 2nd Div. to report to A.D.V.S. A.D.V.S. away inspecting units, collected 15 horses	
	from Division	
24.9.14	Collected 11 more sick horses	
25.9.14	A.D.V.S. visited sick at DHUIZEL & instructed me to await orders as to invalid head.	

War Diary of Captain W.N. Taylor, A.V.C. Vet 2 Cav Bde

Army Form C. 2118.

Instructions regarding War Diaries and Intelligence Summaries are contained in F. S. Regs., Part II. and the Staff Manual respectively. Title pages will be prepared in manuscript.

WAR DIARY
or
INTELLIGENCE SUMMARY.
(Erase heading not required.)

Hour, Date, Place	Summary of Events and Information	Remarks and references to Appendices
11 am 26.9.14. DHUIZEL	Received orders from A.D.V.S. to conduct horses to BRAINE for entrainment.	
12.30 P.M.	Started off with 83 horses.	
2.30 P.M.	Arrival at BRAINE & reported to R.T.O. No trucks available, but infecting an empty train to arrive.	
	Sent orders to stables to await orders.	
8 P.M. 27.9.14. BRAINE	Entrained 81 horses. 2 horses died en route.	
9 am 28.9.14	Returned to DHUIZEL and reports arrival to A.D.V.S.	
29.9.14. DHUIZEL.	Collecting horses from 2nd Div.	
30.9.14 "	" " " "	

12/1812

No 3. Lostile Vety: Lectures

Volume III

Confidential

Vol. 3.

War Diary of Captain W.N. Taylor A.V.C. from 1.10.14 to 31.10.14.

Army Form C. 2118

WAR DIARY
or
INTELLIGENCE SUMMARY. No 2 Mobile Vety Sec.

(Erase heading not required.)

Instructions regarding War Diaries and Intelligence Summaries are contained in F. S. Regs., Part II. and the Staff Manual respectively. Title pages will be prepared in manuscript.

Hour, Date, Place		Summary of Events and Information	Remarks and references to Appendices
1.10.14	DHUIZEL	Infant account of September sent to Hrs. Ordinary work. Collected 8 horses from 2nd Division. One destroyed as being unsafe to move.	
2.10.14	"	Ordinary routine.	
3.10.14	"	Attended 2nd Reg. H.A. Bumont - by Veter. Offr. 2nd Division, sent to Maroue some afternoon. Handed over Section temporarily to Lieut. Handley A.V.C. service H.C.B. Section - no more horses from A.D.V.S.	
4.10.14	"	Ordinary routine	
5.10.14	"	Message received from A.D.V.S. to effect horse from 17th Infy. Bde. white one horse from 17th Infy. Bde.	
6.10.14	"	Received 1013 letter, envelope & wrappings from Division —	
7.10.14	"	Received orders from A.D.V.S. to collect horses on 8.10.14	

WAR DIARY or INTELLIGENCE SUMMARY

(Erase heading not required.)

Army Form C. 2118

Instructions regarding War Diaries and Intelligence Summaries are contained in F. S. Regs., Part II. and the Staff Manual respectively. Title pages will be prepared in manuscript.

Hour, Date, Place	Summary of Events and Information	Remarks and references to Appendices
8.10.14 DHUIZEL	A.D.V.S visited interior. Received verbal instructions re entraining of sick. Collected 79 horses.	
" 7 pm	Received orders from A.D.V.S to conduct all sick horses to Braine. Condition of horse collects seems bad (debilitate)	
9.10.14 7 am	Conducted sick horses to Braine + informed A.D.V.S.	
11.30am BRAINE	Reported to R.T.O. Braine.	
1 pm	Entrained 100 sick horses for Killarmin, St Georges	
2.30 pm	Started for DHUIZEL	
4.30 "	Arrived at DHUIZEL + reported to A.D.V.S.	
10.10.14 DHUIZEL	Forms of clothing to men of sixteen following veterinary services	
11.10.14 "	Received report, march, + picketing lines for entrance.	
12.10 "	Received orders from A.D.V.S re sick horses from this.	

Army Form C. 2118

WAR DIARY
or
INTELLIGENCE SUMMARY.
(Erase heading not required.)

Instructions regarding War Diaries and Intelligence Summaries are contained in F. S. Regs., Part II. and the Staff Manual respectively. Title pages will be prepared in manuscript.

Hour, Date, Place	Summary of Events and Information	Remarks and references to Appendices
13.10.14 6 am DHUIZEL	Received orders from A.D.V.S. to proceed to BRAINE to meet all sick horses & report to O.C. 2nd Div. train, en relieve	
9.30 am	Conducted sick horses to BRAINE	
11.30 am	Arrived at BRAINE & entrained 6 horses	
1 PM	Returned to DHUIZEL & reported to A.D.V.S.	
6 PM	Received confidential orders that section would move at	
	4 am 14.10.14 & march to FÈRE-EN-TARDENOIS.	
14.10.14 4 am	Marched to FÈRE-EN-TARDENOIS	
8 PM	Arrived at FÈRE-EN-TARDENOIS	
11 PM	Entrained en train "E"	
15.10.14	En train	
16.10.14 4 am ST OMER	Reached ST OMER	
11 am	Left by motor march to HAZEBROUCK	
5 PM	Reached HAZEBROUCK	
17.10.14	Discharged from hospital at HAVRE. Received orders to	
	Div. 2 District. Rem. commanded to begin section & proceed	
	HAVRE by 11.39 train.	

WAR DIARY or INTELLIGENCE SUMMARY.

(Erase heading not required.)

Army Form C. 2118.

Instructions regarding War Diaries and Intelligence Summaries are contained in F. S. Regs., Part II. and the Staff Manual respectively. Title pages will be prepared in manuscript.

Hour, Date, Place		Summary of Events and Information	Remarks and references to Appendices
17.10.14.	HAZEBROUCK	Station received orders from Div. sent 10m on 18.10.14, & entrain them at HAZEBROUCK for HAVRE.	
18.10.14		Collected 42 horses and entrained them at HAZEBROUCK at 3 P.M.	
"	3 PM	Received orders from A.D.V.S. to collect 1 horse from 4th S.Amb:lance also one horse from 11th F.C. R.E.	
"	6 PM	Collected 2 horses from 11th F.C. R.E.	
19.10.14.	10 am	Received order to collect all sick horses and run by moto[r] & to entrain same before leaving HAZEBROUCK. Collects & entrained 6 horses for hospital at HAVRE.	
20.10.14.	7.30 am	Rejoined 2nd Divi:sion.	
"	11 am	Arrived at VLAMERTINGHE.	
"	5 PM.	Reached YPRES at 11 PM to rejoin No.3 Mobile Vet: Section.	
"	11 PM	Reported to A.D.V.S at YPRES and took over charge of 3 M.V.S at 11 am, camped about 1 Kilometer W. of YPRES.	
21.10.14.	8.45 am	Section left VLAMERTINGHE for YPRES and camped 1 Kilom: to W. of YPRES.	

WAR DIARY
or
INTELLIGENCE SUMMARY.
(Erase heading not required.)

Army Form C. 2118

Instructions regarding War Diaries and Intelligence Summaries are contained in F. S. Regs., Part II. and the Staff Manual respectively. Title pages will be prepared in manuscript.

Hour, Date, Place		Summary of Events and Information	Remarks and references to Appendices
22.10.14	YPRES.	War diary for Sept & not to A.S's Office	
23.10.14	"	A.D.r.d wants a return. Received order to collect all horses sent on by units. Went to station at YPRES to ascertain facilities for sending away sick horses. Station only used by French Army and R.T.O. of French.	
24.10.14	"	Cable one horse from tower no order from A.D.S. Belongs to 10th Division. Went to Ad 26. 2nd Div & down HQ from Light prepared for Inf. B section. Field art mostly 105 guns.	
25.10.14	"	Received orders from A.D.V.S. 6" Inf Bde. about horse from 6" Inf Bde... some Cavalry. Rect. 6" Inf Bde showing up/km 8 Purpose Hooplogen. Intre with smaller.	
26.10.14	6 PM	Negative reaction. As patient now debilitated & progress unfavourable, it was destroyed. P.D. Joined Unit at Purpura Hooplogen.	

WAR DIARY
or
INTELLIGENCE SUMMARY.
(Erase heading not required.)

Army Form C. 2118

Hour, Date, Place	Summary of Events and Information	Remarks and references to Appendices
27.10.14 YPRES.	Ambulatory & batcases over from 8:17 attend dressing of hospital took over 3 cot cases from Received message from A.D.M.S. to collect 2 horse G. H. 9th R.F.A. Bde unit ship 1 of YPRES. Collected same in the afternoon	
28.10.14 1pm "	Entrained 24 cot cases at YPRES for ABBEVILLE. Admitted 33 men during the afternoon.	
29.10.14 1pm "	Entrained 81 horses at YPRES for ABBEVILLE. 7 horses admitted to M.V.S during the afternoon.	
30.10.14 1pm "	Ordinary routine	
31.10.14 1pm " HPD	Admitted 6 horses Entrained 6 horses with staff of 3rd Cavalry Bde for ABBEVILLE. Marched to a point 1 mile S.E. of VLAMERTINGHE with 2nd Div train Collected 1 horse from H. Feb. Bde.	

II Dn

121/2598

3. Curtuli lectun. AVC.

Vol IV

Nov 1914

Confidential. War Diary of Captain W.N. Taylor AVC from 1·11·14 to 30·11·14 Vol. 4.

Army Form C. 2118.

WAR DIARY
or
INTELLIGENCE SUMMARY.
(Erase heading not required.)

Instructions regarding War Diaries and Intelligence Summaries are contained in F. S. Regs., Part II. and the Staff Manual respectively. Title pages will be prepared in manuscript.

Hour, Date, Place		Summary of Events and Information	Remarks and references to Appendices
1·11·1914	VLAMERTINGHE	Section 1 mile S.E. of VLAMERTINGHE. Despatched important account to Base Remount Depôt, also War Diary for October.	
2·11·14	"	Veterinary routine. Received message from A.D.V.S. wishing of Section. Sent in return cart, horse & bedding. Reported that at present an entire cart wheel was not impounded for government. Collected 2 horses from 26 Bde R.H.A. 1 one from 115th Batter.	
3·11·14	"	Destroyed 1 horse 15" Howitzer, with broken leg.	
4·11·14	"	Entrained 16 horses at POPERINGHE for ABBEVILLE, during the afternoon.	
5·11·14	3 P.M.	Collected 7 horses from 39 Bde. R.F.A. 1st Div. Entrained 13 horses at POPERINGHE for ABBEVILLE. Received authority from 1st Army Corps to increase establishment by 1 cart, horse & driver. This has not been finally arranged.	
6·11·14	"	Admitted 10 horses to section.	

WAR DIARY
or
INTELLIGENCE SUMMARY.
(Erase heading not required.)

Army Form C. 2118.

Instructions regarding War Diaries and Intelligence Summaries are contained in F. S. Regs., Part II. and the Staff Manual respectively. Title pages will be prepared in manuscript.

Hour, Date, Place	Summary of Events and Information	Remarks and references to Appendices
7.11.14. VLAMERTINGHE	Destroyed 1 horse with fractured wheat. Entrained 11 horses at POPERINGHE for ABBEVILLE. One horse from 31 Co A.S.C. with Eczema was sent to ABBEVILLE in isolation as precautionary measure. OC ordered by wire.	
8.11.14 "	Admitted 8 horses. Ordinary routine	
9.11.14 "	Lines visited by ADVS. Admitted 4 horses.	
10.11.14 "	Received message from ADVS re issue of ration by 7 men APC & 4 horses, also message re arrangts for return. Sent message to R.T.O. at POPERINGHE asking for trucks for sick horses & received an answer that trucks were unavailable tomorrow at 2 PM.	
11.11.14 "	Took 17 sick horses to POPERINGHE as arranged with R.T.O. & on arrival found that no trains were available as line had to be cleared of traffic for 48 hours. Returned with sick horse to return until train was ready. Met D.V.S. in POPERINGHE & took over money from Mrs Moore. Distributed articles same evening.	

Army Form C. 2118.

WAR DIARY
or
INTELLIGENCE SUMMARY.
(Erase heading not required.)

Hour, Date, Place	Summary of Events and Information	Remarks and references to Appendices
12.11.14 VLAMERTINGHE	Ordering motors. No trucks available.	
13.11.14 "	Line still closed	
14.11.14 "	Received letter from ADVS re WAGETS conducting railway journies. Went to POPERINGHE to enquire of trucks now available for sick horses.	
15.11.14 "	Entrained 60 horses at POPERINGHE for ABBEVILLE. Admitted 9 others from various Cavalry the afternoon. Weather very wet & cold. Handed over 3 coulets to No 4, 5, + 6, Field Ambulances in substitution from A.DV.S.	
16.11.14 "	A.D.V.S. ordered for all sick men to forward to afternoon Base Veterinary Stores for evenings to regained for 2nd Div.	
17.11.14 "	Sent Pte THOMAS, Army Veterinary Corps to northwest for purpose of proceeding to ABBEVILLE for evenings Ore	

Army Form C. 2118.

WAR DIARY
or
INTELLIGENCE SUMMARY.
(Erase heading not required.)

Instructions regarding War Diaries and Intelligence Summaries are contained in F. S. Regs., Part II. and the Staff Manual respectively. Title pages will be prepared in manuscript.

Hour, Date, Place		Summary of Events and Information	Remarks and references to Appendices
11.30 a.m.	18.11.14 VLAMERTINGHE.	Received verbal order from A.D.V.S. to accompany 2nd Div. trains to the vicinity of HAZEBROUCK.	
1 p.m.	" POPERINGHE	Entrained 21 horses at POPERINGHE STATION for ABBEVILLE. Received verbal order to get out a horse left near POPERINGHE POST-OFFICE; found this horse (2 m.h.y. (a) unable to stand & found it destroyed, and immediately the local police to have it removed. Arrived at HAZEBROUCK 8.30 p.m.	
8.30 p.m.	" HAZEBROUCK		
19.11.14	HAZEBROUCK	Received message from Hd. Qrs. 2nd Div. that 9 men & horses were at HAZEBROUCK to report to. Responded. Went to HAZEBROUCK & conducted them to & fro station. Men found with own blankets & no waterproof sheet. Unable to were submitted to complete their equipment (-) & clothing. Commenced raining during the afternoon & continued heavily during the evening.	
20.11.14	HAZEBROUCK.	Ordinary routine. Hard frost.	
21.11.14	"	Mr. THOMAS returned with Vet. stores from ABBEVILLE. Hard frost.	

(9 29 6) W 3332—1107 100,000 10/13 H W V Forms/C. 2118/10.

Army Form C. 2118.

WAR DIARY
or
INTELLIGENCE SUMMARY.
(Erase heading not required.)

Instructions regarding War Diaries and Intelligence Summaries are contained in F. S. Regs., Part II. and the Staff Manual respectively. Title pages will be prepared in manuscript.

Hour, Date, Place	Summary of Events and Information	Remarks and references to Appendices
22.11.14. HAZEBROUCK.	4 horse keepers & one farrier going sick. First 4 vaccines.	
23.11.14	Snow fry from field cookers & farrier section. Pte HILL, 7 mores went out sick with abscess on arm. Pte BOYD proceeds to ABBEVILLE for Vet stores.	
24.11.14	Pte HILL proceeds to BASE HOSPITAL from CAESTRE station up to 6 pm. Entrained 56 horses at HAZEBROUCK station up to 25.11.14 midnight. 1 N.C.O. + 6 men, all returned to A.D.V.S. visited section during the morning. Weather inclement.	
25.11.14	Ordinary routine. Weather wet. 23 horses (sick) evacuated to section.	
26.11.14	Ordinary routine. Weather wet	
27.11.14	Pte BOYD return from ABBEVILLE with stores. Conducting party returned on 24.11.14 return during the afternoon. Notified A.D.V.S. that registering officer reports unable to find a suitable cart locally. A.D.V.S. advise an affiliated to be made to another regis. Veterinary Officer. Received parcel from Mrs. Moore.	

(9 20 6) W 3332—1107 100,000 10/13 H W V Forms/C. 2118/10.

Army Form C. 2118.

WAR DIARY
or
INTELLIGENCE SUMMARY.

(Erase heading not required.)

Instructions regarding War Diaries and Intelligence Summaries are contained in F.S. Regs., Part II. and the Staff Manual respectively. Title pages will be prepared in manuscript.

Hour, Date, Place	Summary of Events and Information	Remarks and references to Appendices
28.11.14 HAZEBROUCK.	Entrained 40 sick horses at HAZEBROUCK with 1 NCO & 4 men at 2 PM. Pte SHOOBRIDGE admitted to hospital at CAESTRE.	
29.11.14 "	Received Stores & requisites from ADVS, for section. Issued part of it to section. Received rifles in. Lt. Cpt. antoine. Depot Mentioi AVC joined section.	
30.11.14 "	Pte SHOOBRIDGE discharged from hospital & to be reserved duty for two days. Agricultures mill despatched to France & AVR B 158. 3A with horses with section.	

(9 29 6) W 3382—1107 100,000 10/13 H W V Forms/C. 2118/10.

2nd Division

No 3. Mobile Section A.V.C.

Vol VI 1 — 31.12.14

121/4042

Confidential

Vol. V

WAR DIARY
—
INTELLIGENCE SUMMARY.
(Erase heading not required.)

Army Form C. 2118.

Captain W.N. Taylor A.V.C.
from 1st to 31st December 1914.

Instructions regarding War Diaries and Intelligence Summaries are contained in F. S. Regs., Part II. and the Staff Manual respectively. Title pages will be prepared in manuscript.

Hour, Date, Place		Summary of Events and Information	Remarks and references to Appendices
9 a.m.	1.12.14 CAESTRE	41 sick horses with section. Received message from A.D.V.S. reference his inspection of horses announced.	
10 a.m.		One of them died, inspection of mange sent to section from Herts Reg. by Lieut. Williamson.	
	2.12.14 "	Railway conductor to return inspection was belonging to Herts Reg confirmed as Mange. Received confidential instructions from Veranda for "His Majesty" tomorrow.	
	3.12.14 "	Notified A.D.V.S. re his inspection of sick horses for examination & asked for instructions as to disposal of mange case.	
	4.12.14 "	Section visited during morning by D.D.V.S. & A.D.V.S. D.D.V.S. orders destruction of Mange case belonging to Herts Reg. Entrained 53 horses with 1 NCO & 6 men at HAZEBROUCK for ABBEVILLE. Collected ten sick horses off A.C. HAZEBROUCK	
3 P.M.	5.12.14 "	Reported to A.D.V.S. re system of Railway entraining parties & our fetching horses from ADVANCED-BASE-HOSPITALS. Sergt Stambley & Corporal of the section granted leave to ENGLAND from 5.12.14 to midnight 8.12.14.	

Army Form C. 2118.

WAR DIARY
or
INTELLIGENCE SUMMARY.
(Erase heading not required.)

Instructions regarding War Diaries and Intelligence Summaries are contained in F. S. Regs., Part II. and the Staff Manual respectively. Title pages will be prepared in manuscript.

Hour, Date, Place		Summary of Events and Information	Remarks and references to Appendices
	6.12.14 CAESTRE	Ordinary routine	
3 p.m.	7.12.14 "	Moved to point 1 mile North of CAESTRE, to make room for french troops.	
	8.12.14 "	Sergt. Huntley + Comston returned from leave.	
	9.12.14 "	Routine work	
	10.12.14 "	Received message from A.D.V.S. for orderly to report at his office at 8.3 a.m. (11/12/14), also orders to take over and inspect 2nd Divisional train.	
11 a.m.	11.12.14 "	Inspected 2D Co. A.T.C. at BAILLEUL	
3 p.m.		" 11 " " METEREM.	
3.31 p.m.		Met A.D.V.S. on road to CAESTRE	
4 p.m.		A case of skin disease (infectious mange) from 35th Bty R.G.A. admitted to section + treated with Naoline ointment. Admitted two cases suspected of mange from 2nd Divn. Amm. Col. Received instruction from A.D.V.S. re mange cases	

WAR DIARY or INTELLIGENCE SUMMARY.

Army Form C. 2118.

Instructions regarding War Diaries and Intelligence Summaries are contained in F. S. Regs., Part II. and the Staff Manual respectively. Title pages will be prepared in manuscript.

(Erase heading not required.)

Hour, Date, Place		Summary of Events and Information	Remarks and references to Appendices
	12.12.14 CAESTRE	Admitted one lyme case from 2nd Div. Ammn Col. with myst of ichorous about the urethra; referred then to V.6 in charge; took rubbings for examination. Admitted 1 horse from 1st H.L.6 contingent of manage. Two horsekeepers sick and attending hospital. Took over 1 2.D. horse from Ammn Col. to complete establishment of horses. Took over 1 cart & harness from 35 G.A.T.C. to complete establishment.	
9 a.m.	13.12.14 "	D.D.V.S. & A.D.V.S. visited section & ordered change over with section to be destroyed.	
1.30 pm 2 pm	"	Entrained 70 horses for HESDIGNEUL. Isolated one horse of 34th Bde. R.F.A.	
8.30 am	14.12.14 "	Received orders for H.Q.s to be in readiness to move at 2 hours notice from 9 am.	
	15.12.14 "	A.D.V.S. inspected horses belonging to 34th Bdy R.F.A. isolated on 13.12.14. Admitted 2 horses from 31 to H.T.C. suffering of mange.	
2 pm	16.12.14 "	Inspect 35 G.A.T.C.	

Army Form C. 2118.

WAR DIARY
or
INTELLIGENCE SUMMARY.
(Erase heading not required.)

Instructions regarding War Diaries and Intelligence Summaries are contained in F. S. Regs., Part II. and the Staff Manual respectively. Title pages will be prepared in manuscript.

Hour, Date, Place	Summary of Events and Information	Remarks and references to Appendices
17.12.14. CAESTRE	Submitted the following arms inspected & mercoy:— 4 from 5th Bdy. Brig. 6 " 6 " F.A. Ambulance 1 " 20th Coy A.S.C.	
2 pm 18.12.14	Inspected 28 & 11 Coys A.S.C. Embarked & reports himself for duty with Section. 31 horses entrained at HAZEBROUCK for BOULOGNE.	
19.12.14 "	Continue work. Went to HAZEBROUCK & there took over Field Cashier Paul section.	
4 pm 20.12.14 "	Received message from D.A.D.M.S. at HAZEBROUCK that Major Hamilton was sick and would like to see me. Went to HAZEBROUCK & met A.D.V.S. who asked me to conduct the sick cases of 2nd Div. Amm. Col. & 31 Bdy Amm. Col.	
4 pm 21.12.14 "	Inspected invalid cases of 2nd Div. Amm. Col. & 31 Bdy Amm. Col. & handed to A.D.V.S. Railway conducting party entrained from BOULOGNE with horses & pencil from Mrs Moore.	
2 p.m.	6.9 train received orders to be in readiness to move at 7 a.m. 22.12.14. Further orders to follow.	

WAR DIARY or INTELLIGENCE SUMMARY.

Army Form C. 2118.

Hour, Date, Place	Summary of Events and Information	Remarks and references to Appendices
22.12.14. CAESTRE	Marched to HAZEBROUCK & entrained 8 suspected cases of mumps for ABBEVILLE & 16 sick horses for BOULOGNE.	
12 Noon	Saw D.D.V.S. en route. Received message from A.V. & R.M.S. to take over duty of Major Hunter during his illness & to leave all suspicious cases of mange behind & not take any into the new area, also to send in report to A.L. 255 & 2nd Div.	
3. P.M.	Killed 15 horses from 5H "Bty. Amm. Col T.+ H. from Div. Amm Col & in contacts all with suspicious skin disease.	
4 P.M.	Return returned to CAESTRE.	
8.30 a.m. 23.12.14. "	Marched to HAZEBROUCK and arranged to leave the 23 suspected cases of skin disease with no V.C.6 & party, to be entrained at 2.30 P.M. for ABBEVILLE.	
11.30 a.m. "	R.T.O. was notified to " "	
2.30 P.M.	Marched to BETHUNE. Arrival at MERVILLE - from MERVILLE onwards the road was blocked with traffic.	

Army Form C. 2118.

WAR DIARY
or
INTELLIGENCE SUMMARY.
(Erase heading not required.)

Instructions regarding War Diaries and Intelligence Summaries are contained in F. S. Regs., Part II. and the Staff Manual respectively. Title pages will be prepared in manuscript.

Hour, Date, Place		Summary of Events and Information	Remarks and references to Appendices
24.12.14	BETHUNE	Section arrived at about 2 a.m.	
2 a.m.		Reported to Adv. Stn & took over duty of A.D.V.S.	
9 a.m.		Wheel arrival to D.D.V.S.	
		Inspected horses of 6th Field Ambulance.	
25.12.14	"	Admitted 1 case of Strangles from 5th Field Ambulance.	
		Received message from D.D.V.S. wishing for present state of mange & subsequent affected cases.	
		One case of Suspected Influenza in 41st Bty R.F.A.	
26.12.14	"	Reported present state of mange & suspected cases to D.D.V.S. at Gds.	
		Sent suspected case reported from 35th R.G.A.	
		Inspected Divisional troops.	
27.12.14	LOCON	Moved to LOCON with Div. Hd. Qrs. Arrived about 3.30 pm.	
		Section remaining at BETHUNE.	

WAR DIARY or INTELLIGENCE SUMMARY.

(Erase heading not required.)

Army Form C. 2118.

Instructions regarding War Diaries and Intelligence Summaries are contained in F.S. Regs., Part II. and the Staff Manual respectively. Title pages will be prepared in manuscript.

Hour, Date, Place	Summary of Events and Information	Remarks and references to Appendices
9 a.m. 28.12.14. LOCON.	Received message from D.D.V.S. to meet him if possible at Feb. 25 1st Qur. at BETHUNE. Met D.D.V.S. at 10:30 am.	
2 P.M. 3 P.M.	Motored to LE COUTURE and inspected two horses belonging to 34th Bty. which were reported suspicious of mange. Inspected sick horses of 36th Bty. down lot with V.6. Inspected " " " " 41st " " "	
9.30 a.m. 29.12.14.	Went to BOHEME and inspected 4 cases reported as suspicious of mange. These did not appear to be mange cases.	
3 P.M. 3.10 P.M.	Admitted one case of suspicious skin disease from 33rd R.G.A. Admitted 7 mm Sargeon from Meerut Div. Sickom moved to LOCON.	
9.30 a.m. 30.12.14 "	Met Lieut Leveret & inspected nine thin cases sent 31.6.F.R.C. which proved to be "Rangeorn". Afterwards inspected map team belonging to 6th F. Ambulance which were affected with lice.	
1.30 P.M.	Lt. Towe A.V.C. reports himself for duty with 44th Bty R.F.A. He is instructed to report to H.A. 2nd HH Bty R.F.A. at LE-TOURET.	

Army Form C. 2118.

WAR DIARY
or
INTELLIGENCE SUMMARY.
(Erase heading not required.)

Instructions regarding War Diaries and Intelligence Summaries are contained in F. S. Regs., Part II. and the Staff Manual respectively. Title pages will be prepared in manuscript.

Hour, Date, Place	Summary of Events and Information	Remarks and references to Appendices
9.30 am 31.12.14. LOCON	Went to Hd Qtrs Bty. Adv. Dress to inspect some cases reported as suspicious of mumps. Inspected these cases belonging to 114th R.G.A. & ordered them to be sent to section douncester.	
	Went to LA-COUTURE and inspected a suspicious when case reported by N.6 s/c 34th Bty R.F.A. — the case was evacuated to section.	
2.30 pm.	Went to LES LOBES with Lieut. Joure and inspected 6 cases belonging to 114th Bty. 2mm Col which had been isolated for Then disease. One suspicious case was evacuated, others were affected with lice. Noticed that Major Britton was affected ADS 1.	
	1083 milk forms were evacuated by section to 31.12.14	

2nd Division

War Diaries

No 2 Mobile Vety Section

From 1st January, To 30th November 1915

2nd Division $\frac{121}{4330}$

No 3. Mobile Vety Section.

Vol VI.

Confidential

Vol VI

WAR DIARY of ~~No 1~~ Cam WM1 Supply AVC.
or
INTELLIGENCE SUMMARY. for 1.1.15 to 31.1.15.
(Erase heading not required.)

Army Form C. 2118.

Instructions regarding War Diaries and Intelligence Summaries are contained in F. S. Regs., Part II. and the Staff Manual respectively. Title pages will be prepared in manuscript.

Hour, Date, Place		Summary of Events and Information	Remarks and references to Appendices
10 a.m.	1.1.15 LOCON.	Went to BÉTHUNE & inspected 6th Field Ambulance	
12.30 P.M.	"	Inspected 35th C.A.T.C & 11 C.A.T.	
3 P.M.	"	28th C.A.T.C & 31 C.A.T.C.	
	2.1.15	Inspected 24 horses at MV1 for depôt to without at CHOCQUES for NEUCHÂTEL.	
		Sergt. Handley Inspected on transfer to FORGES.	
		Corpls. Daniels & Thomas proceeded on transfer to 2nd q section at	
		ABBEVILLE from CHOCQUES	
		Inspected horses belonging to 2nd Signal Squadron.	
2.30 P.M.		Inspected 35 C.A.T.C.	
10 a.m.	3.1.15	Met Major Isabell AVC, Veterinary ADVS.	
1.30 P.M.		Also took ADV1. to 14th My Amm. Col. to inspect some feed	
2.30 "		cases of oaten chaves which had been reported by V6 Sps.	
		Found several cases suspicious of Navicular Malady, what were	
		conveyed to M.V.1.	
4 P.M.		Went with ADV1. to 2nd Provision & inspected 3 cases of oaten	
		chaves & sent them to M.V.1	

Army Form C. 2118.

WAR DIARY
or
INTELLIGENCE SUMMARY.
(Erase heading not required.)

Instructions regarding War Diaries and Intelligence Summaries are contained in F. S. Regs., Part II. and the Staff Manual respectively. Title pages will be prepared in manuscript.

Hour, Date, Place	Summary of Events and Information	Remarks and references to Appendices
9 am 4.1.15 LOCON	Admitted 15 horses to M.V.S. from 3 A."Bty Amm Col on first of march; also 3 from 2nd Grenadiers.	
12 Noon	Sent 24 unfit to arrange cars to ABBEVILLE from CHOCQUES. Accompanied A.D.V.S. to LE TOURET & LA COUTURE.	
2 PM	Went with A.D.V.S. to PARADIS.	
5.1.15 "	Went with A.D.V.S. to PARADIS & inspected 44" Bty & 36"Hy RHA. Admitted three cases of unafected mange from 44 Bty R.F.A.; seven from 36 Bty R.F.A. & two from 41 Bty R.F.A. Ordered three horses at CHOCQUES.	
10.30 am 6.1.15 "	D.D.V.S. & A.D.V.S. inspected three cars with M.V.S.	
2 PM	Entrained 23 sick horses at CHOCQUES for NEUFCHATEL.	
2.30 PM	Went to Hd. Qrs. T. Bn. & inspected some sore cases with V.O. in charge.	
9.30 am 7.1.15 "	Accompanied A.D.V.S. to ROUBEC to inspect Div. Amm. Col.; found 3 cases suffering of mange.	
2 PM	Inspected 11 G. A.A.C. & 15 G. A.B.C.	
4 PM	Admitted 3 cases of skin disease from Div. Amm. Col. & 2 from 2nd Grenadiers.	

Army Form C. 2118.

WAR DIARY
or
INTELLIGENCE SUMMARY.
(Erase heading not required.)

Instructions regarding War Diaries and Intelligence Summaries are contained in F. S. Regs., Part II. and the Staff Manual respectively. Title pages will be prepared in manuscript.

Hour, Date, Place	Summary of Events and Information	Remarks and references to Appendices
10.30 am 8.1.15. LOCON	Sent 15 other cases & 23 sick horses to CHOCQUES for ABBEVILLE & NEUFCHATEL respectively. One horse was destroyed en route. Inspected 31 & 28 Co. A.T.C.	
2.30 pm.		
9.1.15. "	Went to HINGES to see two horses belonging to 2nd Field Sqdn R.E. Farrier Major Gillman went with.	
10.1.15 "	Inspected horses of 35 & 11 Co. A.T.C. Colomny veterinary.	
9.30 am 11.1.15 "	Inspected sick of 20 Co. A.T.C. Admitted two cases suspicious of mange.	
12.1.15 "	Evacuated 8 cases of impetetis mange at CHOCQUES for ABBEVILLE about 21 sick cases for NEUFCHATEL. Admitted one case of skin disease from 22nd Bty. Sent Drawing for Dec. 14 to A.D.V.S. Officd.	

Army Form C. 2118.

WAR DIARY
or
INTELLIGENCE SUMMARY.
(Erase heading not required.)

Instructions regarding War Diaries and Intelligence Summaries are contained in F. S. Regs., Part II. and the Staff Manual respectively. Title pages will be prepared in manuscript.

Hour, Date, Place		Summary of Events and Information	Remarks and references to Appendices
2 PM	13.1.15 LOCON	D.D.V.S. visited sections. Went to BETHUNE & inspected horses of A & 6th Field Ambulance.	
9.30am	14.1.15 "	Inspected 20 C.A.A.C at PARADIS. Ordinary routine.	
10 am	15.1.15 "	Inspected one charger of 2nd Div. Train to Major Rose A.V.C. three "Homekeepers" for General action.	
	16.1.15 "	Ordinary routine. Down to D.V.O. inspect 6 Field books. Part Section.	
	17.1.15 "	Inspected 8 sham vans at CHOCQUES 15 sick horses	
3 PM	"	Went to HINGES to see horse belonging to 20 C.A.A.C.T ordered it to be destroyed (debilitated.)	
10 am	18.1.15 "	Went to BETHUNE to inspect sick horses of A & 6th Field Amb.	
	19.1.15 "	Inspected horses belonging to East Anglian Fd. RE.	
2.30 PM	"	Entrained 8 sick cases from CHOCQUES for ABBEVILLE 16 sick horses " " " NEUFCHATEL.	

Army Form C. 2118.

WAR DIARY
or
INTELLIGENCE SUMMARY.
(Erase heading not required.)

Instructions regarding War Diaries and Intelligence Summaries are contained in F. S. Regs., Part II. and the Staff Manual respectively. Title pages will be prepared in manuscript.

Hour, Date, Place	Summary of Events and Information	Remarks and references to Appendices
20.1.15 LOCON	Routine work.	
10 a.m. 21.1.15 "	Inspected 5th & 6th Field Ambulances and horses.	
2.30 p.m. 22.1.15 "	Inspected 6th Field Ambulance at BETHUNE	
3 " "	" " "	
10 a.m. 23.1.15 "	Went to BUSNES to collect a horse & found £150 for the Regt. Went 14 mile horses from CHOCQUES to NEUFCHATEL. "Storekeeper" Boar, Raglan & Gladwish with conducting party to No 10 Hospital at NEUFCHATEL.	
12. Noon		
	Received orders to assume charge of Divl. Train	
24.1.15. "	DDVS & ADVS wanted return collected two horses left at NEW CHAPELLE belonging to Warwickshire R.H.A.	
25.1.15 "	Entrained 16 other ranks at CHOCQUES for HESDIGNEUL JUNCTION.	

Army Form C. 2118.

WAR DIARY
or
INTELLIGENCE SUMMARY.
(Erase heading not required.)

Instructions regarding War Diaries and Intelligence Summaries are contained in F. S. Regs., Part II. and the Staff Manual respectively. Title pages will be prepared in manuscript.

Hour, Date, Place	Summary of Events and Information	Remarks and references to Appendices
26.1.15 LOCON.	Four "Housekeepers" arrived for duty.	
27.1.15 "	Entrained 31 horses (Chan division) for HESDIGNEUL at CHOCQUES.	
28.1.15 "	Entrained 40 horses (Chan division) for HESDIGNEUL at CHOCQUES.	
29.1.15 "	D.D.V.J. visited section	
30.1.15 "	Entrained 52 a/km cars + 16 mtr at CHOCQUES. for HESDIGNEUL + NEUFCHATEL respectively. Received orders to move at 1 hour notice.	
31.1.15 "	Routine work.	

Avd

2no Division

121/4508

ko 3 hostile beb.: sektion.

Vol VII.

24/1 1915

① Captain W.W. Taylor A.V.C. Vol. 7.

Army Form C. 2118.

WAR DIARY
or
~~INTELLIGENCE~~ SUMMARY.
(Erase heading not required.)

Instructions regarding War Diaries and Intelligence Summaries are contained in F. S. Regs., Part II. and the Staff Manual respectively. Title pages will be prepared in manuscript.

Hour, Date, Place	Summary of Events and Information	Remarks and references to Appendices
1.2.15 LOCON	Routine work.	
2.2.15 "	A.D.V.S. visited section.	
2 pm. 3.2.15 "	Entrained 16 horses at CHOCQUES for NEUFCHATEL.	
4.2.15 "	Received orders to proceed to BÉTHUNE tomorrow.	
10.30am 5.2.15 BÉTHUNE	Moved section to BÉTHUNE. Received orders to arrange change of 26th Heavy R.G.A. Ammn Col. T. H. 5, & 6th Field Ambulance.	
6.2.15 "	Routine work.	
7.2.15 "	D.D.V.S. visited section	
8.2.15 "	Routine work.	

Army Form C. 2118.

WAR DIARY
or
INTELLIGENCE SUMMARY.
(Erase heading not required.)

Instructions regarding War Diaries and Intelligence Summaries are contained in F. S. Regs., Part II. and the Staff Manual respectively. Title pages will be prepared in manuscript.

Hour, Date, Place	Summary of Events and Information	Remarks and references to Appendices
9.2.15 BÉTHUNE.	Routine work.	
2 pm. 10.2.15	Returned 16 horses at CHOCQUES for NEUFCHATEL.	
11.2.15	Went to BEUVRY to inspect a horse which had been left with a farmer during November.	
12.2.15	D.D.V.J. visited section.	
13.2.15	Went to FOUQUERES to inspect a horse which had been left with a farmer since 29th Oct. 14. Collected one horse from BEUVRY.	
2 pm "	Entrained 16 sick horses at CHOCQUES for NEUFCHATEL.	
14.2.15 "	Collected 1 horse from FOUQUERES.	
15.2.15 "	Routine work.	
16.2.15 "	Paid section.	
17.2.15 "	Routine work.	

Army Form C. 2118.

WAR DIARY
or
INTELLIGENCE SUMMARY.
(Erase heading not required.)

Instructions regarding War Diaries and Intelligence Summaries are contained in F. S. Regs., Part II. and the Staff Manual respectively. Title pages will be prepared in manuscript.

Hour, Date, Place	Summary of Events and Information	Remarks and references to Appendices
2 P.M. 18.2.15 BÉTHUNE	Entrained 16 m/k horses for NEUFCHATEL.	
19.2.15 "	Routine work	
20.2.15 "	Routine work.	
21.2.15 "	Admitted 6 cases of skin disease from 36th Bty. R.F.A.	
22.2.15 "	Routine work.	
23.2.15 "	Entrained 16 m/k horses at BÉTHUNE for NEUFCHATEL.	
24.2.15 "	Routine work	
25.2.15 "	Entrained 16 m/k horses at BÉTHUNE for NEUFCHATEL.	
26.2.15 "	Routine work.	

2nd Division

bis 3. mobili Vetg: Lectur.

Vol VIII 1 — 31.3.15

Vol. 8.

Confidential

Captain W.N. Dunford. RAMC   Army Form C. 2118.

WAR DIARY
or
INTELLIGENCE SUMMARY.
(Erase heading not required.)

Hour, Date, Place	Summary of Events and Information	Remarks and references to Appendices
9 am 1.3.15. BÉTHUNE	Routine work.	
	Went to CROIX MARMEUSE to arrange belonging to 34" Bty R.F.A. + arranged for an ambulance to convey it to Mobile Section	
2.3.15	D.D.M.S. visited unit.	
10 am 3.3.15	16 rank & file were entrained at BÉTHUNE for MANCHESTER. Sent ambulance to CROIX MARMEUSE to fetch change belonging to 3rd (City) R.F.A. Routine work.	
4.3.15	Routine work.	
5.3.15	Sent first Routinerien reported for duty	
6.3.15	Routine work.	
7.3.15	Two horses sent to No 3 Remount Depot, BOULOGNE from BÉTHUNE.	
8.3.15	Billeted one horse from LA BEUVRE	

WAR DIARY
or
INTELLIGENCE SUMMARY.
(Erase heading not required.)

Army Form C. 2118.

Instructions regarding War Diaries and Intelligence Summaries are contained in F. S. Regs., Part II. and the Staff Manual respectively. Title pages will be prepared in manuscript.

Hour, Date, Place	Summary of Events and Information	Remarks and references to Appendices
10 am 9.3.15 BETHUNE	Entrained 24 mth horses at BETHUNE for NEUCHATEL.	
10.3.15 "	Routine work.	
11.3.15 "	Entrained 15 mth horses at BETHUNE for NEUFCHATEL.	
12.3.15 "	Routine work.	
13.3.15 "	Routine work.	
14.3.15 "	Routine work.	
10 am 15.3.15 "	24 Pack horses entrained at BETHUNE for NEUFCHATEL.	
16.3.15 "	Routine work.	
17.3.15 "	16 mth horses entrained for NEUFCHATEL at BETHUNE.	
18.3.15 "	Routine work.	

Army Form C. 2118.

WAR DIARY
or
INTELLIGENCE SUMMARY.
(Erase heading not required.)

Instructions regarding War Diaries and Intelligence Summaries are contained in F. S. Regs., Part II. and the Staff Manual respectively. Title pages will be prepared in manuscript.

Hour, Date, Place	Summary of Events and Information	Remarks and references to Appendices
19.3.15 BETHUNE	To transit 16 horses at BETHUNE for NEUFCHATEL. Capt. Shurbridge sick & goes to hospital.	
20.2.15 "	Routine work.	
21.3.15 "	Went to CHOCQUES to enquire of sick horses belonging to 1st Queens. They & rest three of them to N.V.S.	
22.3.15 "	4 men on fowl in transit at CHOCQUES for No 3-Shawn to Dépôt, BOULOGNE.	
23.3.15 "	Farrier Sgt Williams admitted sick to hospital.	
24.3.15 "	Routine work.	
25.3.15 "	Entrained 16 sick horses at BETHUNE for NEUFCHATEL.	
26.3.15 "	Routine work.	
27.3.15 "	Cheque for 38.05 fr. from 2nd in Transport Issued returned to D.S.T.	

Army Form C. 2118.

WAR DIARY
or
INTELLIGENCE SUMMARY.
(Erase heading not required.)

Instructions regarding War Diaries and Intelligence Summaries are contained in F. S. Regs., Part II. and the Staff Manual respectively. Title pages will be prepared in manuscript.

Hour, Date, Place	Summary of Events and Information	Remarks and References to Appendices
28.3.15 BETHUNE	3 Men on fork entrained at CHOCQUES for No. 3 Remount Depôt BOULOGNE. 16 cart horses entrained at BETHUNE for NEUFCHATEL.	
29.3.15	Routine work.	
30.3.15	Routine work.	
31.3.15	Routine work. 7 p.m. Gent. sent off for trials in vicinity of we have no remarks.	

121/5256

2ᵈ Division

bis 3. hrtil Vetg: sectin

Vol IX 1 — 30.4.15.

Vol. 2.

No 3 MOBILE VETERINARY SECTION.

Confidential. Captain W.N. Taylor. A.V.C.

Army Form C. 2118.

WAR DIARY
or
INTELLIGENCE SUMMARY.
(Erase heading not required.)

Instructions regarding War Diaries and Intelligence Summaries are contained in F. S. Regs, Part II. and the Staff Manual respectively. Title pages will be prepared in manuscript.

Hour, Date, Place	Summary of Events and Information	Remarks and References to Appendices
10 AM. 1.4.15. BÉTHUNE.	Entrained 16 sick horses at BÉTHUNE for NEUFCHATEL. Sent to 1015 N.E. to complete two horses left in charge of farrier.	
2.4.15 "	Took over Veterinary charge of 2nd Squadron from from Major Rose A.V.C. who is proceeding to England on duty. Inspected 25, 28, N, & 31 Cos. M.V.C. Routine work.	
3.4.15 "	Routine work.	
4.4.15 "	Entrained 24 sick horses at BÉTHUNE for NEUFCHATEL. Collected two horses from Loubon Rotté of LOISNE.	
5.4.15 "	Collected one horse from M. Lecour of ANNEZIN.	
6.4.15 "	Routine work.	
7.4.15 "	Routine work.	
8.4.15 "	Inspected 2nd Div. Train	

Army Form C. 2118.

WAR DIARY
or
INTELLIGENCE SUMMARY.
(Erase heading not required.)

Hour, Date, Place	Summary of Events and Information	Remarks and References to Appendices
9.4.15 BETHUNE.	Pontoon work.	
10.4.15 "	Entrained 16 hours at BETHUNE for NEUFCHATEL.	
11.4.15 "	Entrained 6 hours in fact at CHOCQUES for No. 4 Remount Depot, BOULOGNE. Pontoon work.	
12.4.15 "	Pontoon work.	
13.4.15 "	Pontoon work.	
14.4.15 "	D.V.S. visited section.	
15.4.15 "	D.V.S. completed section. 3 horses in fact entrained at CHOCQUES for No. 4 Remount Depot BOULOGNE. Pontoon work.	
16.4.15 "	Pontoon work.	
17.4.15 "	Inflated one horse from M. Maurel Dairies of HINGES. Received new limber wagon & handed over cart at CHOCQUES.	

Vol. 9

Army Form C. 2118.

WAR DIARY
or
INTELLIGENCE SUMMARY.
(Erase heading not required.)

Instructions regarding War Diaries and Intelligence Summaries are contained in F. S. Regs., Part II. and the Staff Manual respectively. Title pages will be prepared in manuscript.

Hour, Date, Place	Summary of Events and Information	Remarks and References to Appendices
18.4.15. BETHUNE.	Transferred men to New Billet.	
19.4.15 "	Routine work.	
20.4.15 "	Road section	
21.4.15. "	Entrained 14 horses at BETHUNE for NEUFCHATEL.	
22.4.15 "	Transferred men to other billet to make room for 2nd L/Div.	
23.4.15 "	Routine work. DDVS visited section.	
24.4.15 "	Routine work. Destroyed horse in quarantine sick.	
25.4.15 "	Entrained 16 horses at BETHUNE for NEUFCHATEL.	
26.4.15 "	Inspected 2nd Div. horses	

Vol. 9

Army Form C. 2118.

WAR DIARY
or
INTELLIGENCE SUMMARY.
(Erase heading not required.)

Instructions regarding War Diaries and Intelligence Summaries are contained in F.S. Regs., Part II. and the Staff Manual respectively. Title pages will be prepared in manuscript.

Hour, Date, Place	Summary of Events and Information	Remarks and References to Appendices
27.4.15 BÉTHUNE	Went to ESSAR to what a suitable place for collecting station	
28.4.15 "	Entrained 15 horses at BÉTHUNE for NEUFCHATEL. Entrained 3 mares in foal & 1 mare with a foal at CHOCQUES for the A. Remount Depôt BOULOGNE	
29.4.15 "	Despatched 1 horse belonging to 41st Bdy. RFA with injury to back. Cant cart near station	
30.4.15 "	Routine work.	

121/5336

2nd Division

No 3. Ludhila Vity Station

Part 1 — 31.5.15.

Vol X

Army Form C. 2118.

WAR DIARY of Capt. W.R. Taylor A.V.C.
O.C. No 2 M.V.S.

or

INTELLIGENCE SUMMARY.

(Erase heading not required.)

Hour, Date, Place	Summary of Events and Information	Remarks and References to Appendices
1.5.15 BETHUNE.	Routine work.	
2.5.15 "	Inspected 2nd Div. Horses.	
3.5.15 "	Routine work.	
4.5.15 "	Inspected horses of 2nd Div. Train.	
5.5.15 " 2 pm	Corporal Golding A.V.C. reports for duty. Evacuated 16 sick horses for NEUFCHATEL at BETHUNE.	
6.5.15 "	Routine work.	
7.5.15 "	A/Sergt. Topham A.V.C. transferred to No. 3 Veterinary Hospital BOULOGNE. Formed an advanced collecting station at ESSAR.	
8.5.15 "	Removed a mule & foal belonging to 60 Bty from No. 2 M.V.Sec LOCON.	

Army Form C. 2118.

WAR DIARY
or
INTELLIGENCE SUMMARY.
(Erase heading not required.)

Instructions regarding War Diaries and Intelligence Summaries are contained in F. S. Regs., Part II. and the Staff Manual respectively. Title pages will be prepared in manuscript.

Hour, Date, Place	Summary of Events and Information	Remarks and References to Appendices
9.5.15 BETHUNE	Entrained one more & four & one more in four at BETHUNE for No. 1 Remount Depot, BOULOGNE.	
10.5.15 "	Removed advanced collecting station at LA-TOURET. Impacted 2nd Div train. Continued work.	
11.5.15 "		
12.5.15 " 2 P.M.	Entrained 16 mule horses at BETHUNE for NEUFCHATEL. Removed section to LOCON.	
13.5.15 LOCON	Second advanced collecting station on road 1 kilom to S. of LA COUTURE. Inspected Div. train.	
14.5.15 "	Sergt Stafford A.V.C. reports himself for duty on transfer from No. 2 N.V.A. Horse-keeper Dicks sent sick with dog bite.	
15.5.15 "	Continued work.	

Army Form C. 2118.

WAR DIARY
or
INTELLIGENCE SUMMARY.
(Erase heading not required.)

Instructions regarding War Diaries and Intelligence Summaries are contained in F.S. Regs., Part II. and the Staff Manual respectively. Title pages will be prepared in manuscript.

Hour, Date, Place	Summary of Events and Information	Remarks and References to Appendices
16.5.15 LOCON	14 sick horses evacuated at BÉTHUNE for ABBEVILLE. 1 horse in foal evacuated to No. 2 Remount Depôt, ABBEVILLE.	
17.5.15 "	Inspected Div. Train.	
18.5.15 "	Routine work.	
19.5.15 "	Evacuated 20 sick horses at CHOCQUES for ABBEVILLE. 3 mares in foal at " " No 2. Depôt ABBEVILLE.	
20.5.15 "	Routine work.	
21.5.15 "	Routine work.	
22.5.15 " 3 P.M	Inspected 35.9.14 to A.D.C. Destroyed 3 horses at Abattoir, BÉTHUNE.	
23.5.15 "	Routine work.	
24.5.15 "	Routine work.	

(9 29 6) W 3332—1107 100,000 10/13 H W V Forms/C. 2118/10.

Army Form C. 2118.

WAR DIARY
or
INTELLIGENCE SUMMARY.
(Erase heading not required.)

Instructions regarding War Diaries and Intelligence
Summaries are contained in F. S. Regs., Part II.
and the Staff Manual respectively. Title pages
will be prepared in manuscript.

Hour, Date, Place	Summary of Events and Information	Remarks and References to Appendices
25.5.15 LOCON	Marching orders & route march from 11 a.m to 12.30 P.M.	
26.5.15 "	Entrained 23 sick horses at CHOCQUES & 1 mare in foal for ABBEVILLE.	
27.5.15 "	Entrained 4 cases of skin diseases at CHOCQUES for ABBEVILLE.	
28.5.15 " 5 a.m	March to AMES arriving about 9 a.m & reported arrival to O.C. 60th Bde for billeting area. Billet at AMES.	
29.5.15. AMES	Rode to LILLERS to arrange for evacuation of sick horses. Collected one horse from Maurice of LIERES left with him on 25.5.15 by Mons Bosquila, 2nd Ind. C. Div.	
30.5.15 "	Routine work.	
31.5.15 "	Nail ox turn. Entrained 21 sick horses at LILLERS for ABBEVILLE.	

2nd Division

ho 3 herbil Vetg: Sector

Jul XI 1—30.6.15

(1.)

Vol XI

C.C. No. 3 Mobile Veterinary Section.
Captain W. H. Jasper A.V.C.

Confidential

Army Form C. 2118.

WAR DIARY
INTELLIGENCE SUMMARY.
(Erase heading not required.)

Instructions regarding War Diaries and Intelligence Summaries are contained in F. S. Regs., Part II. and the Staff Manual respectively. Title pages will be prepared in manuscript.

Hour, Date, Place	Summary of Events and Information	Remarks and References to Appendices
1.6.15. AMES.	Routine work.	
2.6.15. "	"	
3.6.15. "	"	
4.6.15. "	Admitted 3 cases of skin disease from 36th Bty. R.F.A. (unfit to march)	
5.6.15. "	P.D.V.S. inspected the above when came under section.	
2 A.M. 6.6.15.	Entrained 12 cases of unfit to march of LITTERS for ABBEVILLE	
4 P.M. "	Went to Mons de Merles, Soue No. 7 à AUCHEL and inspected & destroyed one horse with open back wound left by a "Siege Battery on 3.6.15.	
7.6.15. "	Admitted 5 cases of skin disease from 36th Bty. Open Col.	
2.6.15. "	Entrained 5 skin cases & 9 ordinary cases of LITTERS for ABBEVILLE. Received orders to move section to HESDIGNEUL, tomorrow.	
3 P.M.		

Army Form C. 2118.

WAR DIARY
or
INTELLIGENCE SUMMARY.
(Erase heading not required.)

Instructions regarding War Diaries and Intelligence Summaries are contained in F. S. Regs., Part II. and the Staff Manual respectively. Title pages will be prepared in manuscript.

Hour, Date, Place	Summary of Events and Information	Remarks and references to Appendices
8.30am 9.6.15. AMES	Left AMES & route march for HESDIGNEUL. Collected 1 horse from Walls Arthur & 102INGHEM. Left with him on 30.5.15 by O.C. M.h.Co. 2nd Div. Train. Arrived at HESDIGNEUL :-	
12. Noon		
10.6.15 HESDIGNEUL	Routine work.	
11.6.15 "	Nowt return	
12.6.15 "	Collected one horse left with infft. Folkham at AUCHEL by O.C. H. 2nd Co. of 2nd Div. Train.	
2 p.m. 13.6.15 "	Entrained HP horses at CHOCQUES for ABBEVILLE including 2 incomplete remounts & 15 for remount the first from 2nd Div. Ammn Col.	
14.6.15 "	Inspected 2nd Div. Train.	
15.6.15 "	" "	
16.6.15 "	Routine work.	
17.6.15 "	O.X.V of moral section	

Army Form C. 2118.

WAR DIARY
or
INTELLIGENCE SUMMARY.
(Erase heading not required.)

Instructions regarding War Diaries and Intelligence Summaries are contained in F. S. Regs., Part II. and the Staff Manual respectively. Title pages will be prepared in manuscript.

Hour, Date, Place	Summary of Events and Information	Remarks and references to Appendices
18.6.15 HESDIGNEUL	Obtained 21 horses at CHOCQUES including 5 complete changes.	
19.6.15 "	Routine work	
20.6.15 "	Ptes. Douglas, Northey & Wheeler at fork Thursdays for duty.	
21.6.15 "	Routine work	
22.6.15 "		
23.6.15 "	" "	
24.6.15 "	Entrained Ponturing & Potter Lorries at CHOCQUES for ABBEVILLE.	
25.6.15 "	Routine work	
26.6.15 "	" "	
27.6.15 "	" "	
2.30 PM 28.6.15 "	Moved motor to BETHUNE.	
2 PM "	Entrained 16 horses at CHOCQUES for ABBEVILLE.	
29.6.15 BETHUNE	Inspection 2nd Div. Train.	
30.6.15 "	Capt. B. HESDIGNEUL & inspected 8 horses left behind by 2nd Div. Train.	

12/
6973

2nd Division

2o S. Mobile Telg: Section

Vol XLI

July August & Sept 15

Ans

Vol. XII

Army Form C. 2118.

WAR DIARY of Officer Commanding No 3 Mobile Veterinary Section

or

INTELLIGENCE SUMMARY

(Erase heading not required.)

Instructions regarding War Diaries and Intelligence Summaries are contained in F. S. Regs., Part II. and the Staff Manual respectively. Title pages will be prepared in manuscript.

Hour, Date, Place	Summary of Events and Information	Remarks and references to Appendices
1.7.15 BETHUNE	Inspected 2nd Div. Train.	
2.7.15 "	Rest section.	
3.7.15 "	Routine work	
4.7.15 "	"	
5.7.15 "	Inspected 2nd Div. Train	
6.7.15 "	Routine work.	
7.7.15 "	Entrained 15 horses at BETHUNE for ABBEVILLE.	
8.7.15 "	Routine work.	
9.7.15 "	"	
10.7.15 "	"	
11.7.15 "	"	
12.7.15 "	"	
13.7.15 "	Inspected train. Collected own horses from M. Lica. to VERDIN, sent unknown.	
14.7.15 "	Entrained filling parried to ABBEVILLE for course of instruction. Entrained 8 sick horses at BETHUNE for ABBEVILLE.	

Army Form C. 2118.

WAR DIARY
or
INTELLIGENCE SUMMARY.
(Erase heading not required.)

Instructions regarding War Diaries and Intelligence Summaries are contained in F. S. Regs., Part II. and the Staff Manual respectively. Title pages will be prepared in manuscript.

Hour, Date, Place	Summary of Events and Information	Remarks and references to Appendices
15.7.15. BETHUNE.	Inspected Troops.	
16.7.15 "	Routine work.	
17.7.15 "	"	
18.7.15 "	Colonel Saunders granted 7 days leave to England.	
19.7.15 "	Inspected Troops.	
20.7.15 "	Major Robin proceeded to ETAPLES on leave took over his duties temporarily.	
21.7.15 "	Evacuation of 13 horses at ETAPLES for ABBEVILLE.	
22.7.15 "	Routine work.	
23.7.15 "	Inspected Troops.	
24.7.15 "	Colonel Pickling returned to duty from No 5 Veterinary Hospital, ABBEVILLE.	
25.7.15 "	Attended Field Holdings Commission of another Listing of horses (grenades).	

Army Form C. 2118.

WAR DIARY
or
INTELLIGENCE SUMMARY.

(Erase heading not required.)

Instructions regarding War Diaries and Intelligence Summaries are contained in F. S. Regs., Part II. and the Staff Manual respectively. Title pages will be prepared in manuscript.

Hour, Date, Place	Summary of Events and Information	Remarks and references to Appendices
26.7.15. BETHUNE.	Employed in training 9.2" Howitzer Pers.	
27.7.15. "	Employed Training.	
28.7.15. "	Captain Taylor A.V.C. proceeded to England.	

Vol I

WAR DIARY
or
INTELLIGENCE SUMMARY.
(Erase heading not required.)

Army Form C. 2118.

Of Officer Commanding 3 Mob Vet Sect

Hour, Date, Place	Summary of Events and Information	Remarks and references to Appendices
5/8/15 Bethune	Lieut D.G.S. Beck AVC appointed to the Command. Routine work	D.G.S.B.
6/8/15 Bethune	Lieut Beck reported his arrival to A.D.V.S. 2nd Division. Routine work. Paid section + both over command of the section.	D.G.S.B.
7/8/15 Bethune	O.C. took over charge 12nd Division horse from Lieut Dunlop A.V.C. Then the section commenced to receive our own daily manuelin & rifle drill. 5 L.D. 5 sgt & 2nd Highland Field Coys. Re Inspected. Routine work.	D.G.S.B.
8/8/15 Bethune	Drivers Wade A.S.C. (attached to section) became to England on 7 days leave. Routine work.	D.G.S.B.
9.8.15 Bethune	Lieut Beck AVC handed over his 3 M.V.S. to Lieut Turner AVC SR & proceeded to Laban Division D.A.C. Sect.	
	Took over charge from Lt. Beck AVC.	
10/8/15 "	Pte Maker admitted to hospital	L.P.Turner
	Took over charge of No.11 Derot Team. Routine work. Evacuated 9 mules & 1 horse at Choques	
11/8/15 "	Inspected 5-5 S.A. Fld Co. R.E. & 2 Hghld Co.R.E. & others. Routine work & rifle drill	L.P.Turner
12/8/15 "	Inspected Nº 2 Divl Train. Routine work.	L.P.Turner
13/8/15 "	Inspected horses sent from 2nd Divl Train & removed section. Routine work.	"
14/8/15 "	Routine work. Operated on horse for colour gk. Section inspection rifle drill.	"

Army Form C. 2118.

WAR DIARY
or
INTELLIGENCE SUMMARY.
(Erase heading not required.)

Vol. II

Instructions regarding War Diaries and Intelligence Summaries are contained in F. S. Regs., Part II. and the Staff Manual respectively. Title pages will be prepared in manuscript.

Hour, Date, Place	Summary of Events and Information	Remarks and references to Appendices
15/8/15 Lekhen	Inspection 5th, 5th, 4th & 2nd Regt Red Cresc & 2nd Bul kan hosp. Routine work. Inspected 2nd did ban hosp on hrs destroyed at station.	1st Div.
16/8/15 "	Evacuated 7 hors & one mule at Cherzu	"
17/8/15 "	an hour returned. 2 fowl hosp mores the Bongham sent out ambulance wagons after. Routine work. one horse destroyed yt. infected animal joined & sold & the Lehrn.	1st Div.
18/8/15 "	Routine work. Inspected 2nd Red Cres. two hors returned & m.m.D vent. the bitton destroyed horse belonging to 2 nd Regt. C. Bul 11/94.	1st Div.
19/8/15 "	Routine work. Inspected 2nd Bul train destroyed horse belonging to 2 nd Light. C. Bul 1192.	2 & Spearn
20/8/15 "	Routine work. Inspected 2nd Bul train.	3 & Sprien
21/8/15 "	Routine work, refer inspection & drill	7 & Div.
22/8/15 "	Routine work, evacuated 14 horses & 3 mules	2 & Div.
23/8/15 "	Routine work general fatigue wood yard	" 2 & Div.
24/8/15 "	Inspected 1st Red train lectures work & drill sent in nomination for promotion.	2 Div.
25/8/15 "	Routine work	1st Div.
26/8/15 "	Routine work, cavalry drill & skirmish	
27/8/15 "	Routine work	

Army Form C. 2118.

WAR DIARY
or
INTELLIGENCE SUMMARY
(Erase heading not required.)

Vol III

Hour, Date, Place	Summary of Events and Information	Remarks and references to Appendices
28/8/15	Ampter work. 18 horses & 1 mule evacuated for change.	
29/8/15	Routine work.	
30/8/15	An. Sick out charge No. B hr. S. then Lieut Dimeo Violis 4/2 Engrs RFA horselines and Horse S. Lieut Coyart 1/1st Herts accompanied by him. Dimeo sules takes over groomings. Routinework.	VRRR
31/8/15	Visits /r Lants M/gR horselines and inspects Routine work.	
1/9/15	Routine work. Changing horselines Violis Du man horse line Du in Sid out 19th and 19th Ambulance horse line.	VRRR
2/9/15	Routine work R. Violis horseline in my charge. Continue to line until Curtin.	VRRR
3/9/15	Routine work. Visits Div. horse line within my charge.	VRRR

Army Form C. 2118.

WAR DIARY
or
INTELLIGENCE SUMMARY.
(Erase heading not required.)

Instructions regarding War Diaries and Intelligence Summaries are contained in F. S. Regs., Part II. and the Staff Manual respectively. Title pages will be prepared in manuscript.

Hour, Date, Place	Summary of Events and Information	Remarks and references to Appendices
3/9/15	Routine work. Forecasts advance. Collecting details. Generals visited two of our Divns from.	MRGR
4/9/15	Routine work. Generals 15 horses as 5 mls. Generals visited 15 horses both went	MRGR
5/9/15	Keep change Dr. G. & 2 Dn horses visits 2 Dn Ma. Routine work. Visits all units in my charge.	MRGR
6/9/15	Afternoon.	MRGR
7/9/15	Routine work. Met preparation for hurry to new location. Visited Dr S. and Dn own	MRGR
8/9/15	Changed location. Visited Dr. G. see train bus. Also visit units my charge.	MRGR
9/9/15	Routine work. Visited units in my charge. Hauling Rifles for front styles.	MRGR
10/9/15	Routine work. Hauling Rifle Visits K Gen ... and ... engineers.	MRGR
11/9/15	Routine work. Wilderswhi. Walk as shaking Rifle. Visits Dn train	MRGR

Army Form C. 2118.

WAR DIARY
or
INTELLIGENCE SUMMARY.
(Erase heading not required.)

Instructions regarding War Diaries and Intelligence Summaries are contained in F. S. Regs., Part II. and the Staff Manual respectively. Title pages will be prepared in manuscript.

Hour, Date, Place	Summary of Events and Information	Remarks and references to Appendices
11/5/15	Routine work. Harling Rifle Range. Visits Horse Lines in morning. Inoculation of Horses & Mules.	
12/5/15	Routine work.	
13/5/15	Routine work. Harling Rifle Range. Whitechurch Wall. Jusselin Rifle Garden an	
14/5/15	Rifle Range. Routine work. Harling Range. Visits.	
15/5/15	Routine work. Harling Range. On leave home.	
16/5/15	Rifle Range. Harling Range. Speech Sgt. Blackwell V.S. from Brigade. Awaiting orders. Routine work. Musketry exercise Harling Range	
17/5/15	Routine work. Speech Rifle Range. Leaving. Visits Horse Lines Pit Hill A.V.C. Attached to 17 M.S. awaiting orders.	

(9 29 6) W 3332—1107 100,000 10/13 H W V Forms/C. 2118/10.

WAR DIARY
INTELLIGENCE SUMMARY.
(Erase heading not required.)

Army Form C. 2118.

Hour, Date, Place	Summary of Events and Information	Remarks and references to Appendices
18/9/15	Routine work. Movements of horses to Rosières various ranchères	ADMS
19/9/15	Routine work. Dogs—brikers.	ADMS
20/9/15	Routine work. Rapts to advance clearing station. The ADS at Dr Sogl. Sgt Stapleton Nurse Sgt S. of Laterieur. Visits 2nd Dn. Routine work. Movements 37 horses to	ADMS
21/9/15	Routine work. Attends ogs. Horse changes.	ADMS
22/9/15	Survey night. Visits 3rd Kavy/Compte flu orders travel ridden to provis reg. on man supplies to	ADMS
23/9/15	Routine work. Visits Dr Moreux.	ADMS
24/9/15	Routine work. Horrors change. occurring. AD & ADS 11.30 pm. After lunch and ADS to & ADS 11.30 pm.	ADMS

WAR DIARY
or
INTELLIGENCE SUMMARY.

(Erase heading not required.)

Army Form C. 2118.

Hour, Date, Place	Summary of Events and Information	Remarks and references to Appendices
25/9/15	Routine work. Visits ??? train horse lines. Evacuated 19 horses and 4 mules. Routine work. Grapnels. Billets.	[illegible]
26/9/15	" Evacuated 13 horses [?] 9 mules	[illegible]
27/9/15	" Visits ??? 12 "	[illegible]
28/9/15	Grapnels Rfle. Routine work. Visits ???	[illegible]
29/9/15	train horse lines. Evacuated 14 horses. Routine work. Grapnels on horse lines.	[illegible]
30/9/15	Evacuated 11 horses. Visits train horse lines.	[illegible]
1/10/15	Evacuated 5 horses. Routine work. Visits to train horse lines.	[illegible]
2/10/15	Evacuated 1 horse. Slaughtered horse.	[illegible]

121/7466

2nd Bahrain

3rd Mobile Vac. Secn.

Oct - 15

Vol XIII

Army Form C. 2118.

WAR DIARY of No. 10 Mobile Veterinary Section
3rd Division
by E. Lovell, M.R.C.V.S.
O.C. Ft 7. M.V.S.

INTELLIGENCE SUMMARY. No. 1
(Erase heading not required.)

Instructions regarding War Diaries and Intelligence Summaries are contained in F.S. Regs, Part II. and the Staff Manual respectively. Title pages will be prepared in manuscript.

Hour, Date, Place	Summary of Events and Information	Remarks and references to Appendices
In the Field 1.10.15 At Poperinghe 2.10.15	Section marched to Poperinghe & entrained 91 horses for advanced Veterinary Hosp Ptl 14 hours remaining.	
"	Collecting Post 2 sick horses admitted. 2 horses evacuated S.E. No. 6205 Pte. Laing W., S.E. No. 5075 Tinson W. Joined Section from No. 29 Mobile Veterinary Section 17th Division.	
" 3.10.15	14 horses remaining. Collecting Post. 3 horses admitted. 3 horses evacuated. 14 horses remaining.	
" 4.10.15	Destroyed under arms by Bdr. Bryde. No. S.E. 1960 Pte. Clissold H. reported Collecting Post. Section Medical officer at Rifle Range; S.E. No. 1960 Pte Clissold H. reported. 14 horses remaining.	
" 5.10.15	Collecting Post. 1 horse admitted. 1 horse evacuated. 14 horses remaining.	
" 6.10.15	Collecting Post. 11 horses admitted. 1 received award. 1 horse also forged S.E. No. 1960 Pte Clissold H. awarded 21 days Field Punishment No. 1. 23 horses remaining. Section was inspected by A.D.V.S. 2nd Army.	
" 7.10.15	Collecting Post. 4 horses admitted. 27 horses remaining. No. 25192 Pte MacDonald R admitted to hospital, 4 horses evacuated.	
" 8.10.15	Collecting Post. 3 horses admitted. Section marched to Poperinghe & entrained 14 horses for advanced Veterinary Hospital. 14 horses remaining.	
" 9.10.15	Collecting Post. 2 horses received and. 1 horse evacuated. 13 horses remaining.	
" 10.10.15	Collecting Post. 1 horse died. S.E. No. 6205 Pte. Laing W. admitted to hospital, & evacuated.	

WAR DIARY

INTELLIGENCE SUMMARY. No. 2.

of No. 11 Mobile Veterinary Section, 3rd Division

by E. Lovell, Capt. A.V.C., o.i/c. 11.M.V.S.

Army Form C. 2118

(Erase heading not required.)

Hour, Date, Place	Summary of Events and Information	Remarks and references to Appendices
at Popringhe. 11.10.15	Collecting Sect. 12 horses remaining	
" 12.10.15	Collecting Sect. 27 horses admitted. 39 horses remaining. S.E. No. 833 Pte. Jones.S.A. proceeded to England on leave.	
" 13.10.15	Collecting Sect. 4 horses admitted. 43 horses remaining.	
" 14.10.15	Collecting Sect. 3 horses admitted. 27 Sick & Cast horses evacuated to No. 1 Advanced Veterinary Hospital. 2 horses received and 16 horses remaining. No. 497 Pte. Laws.J. from Field Corporal at No.5 Field Veterinary. No. 36. G.H.Q. TA Echelon. 11.10.15	
" 15.10.15	Collecting Sect. 2 horses admitted. 3 m. received. Collecting Sect. 15 horses remaining.	
" 16.10.15	Collecting Sect. 15 horses remaining.	
" 17.10.15	Collecting Sect. 1 horse admitted. 1 horse received and. 15 horses remaining.	
" 18.10.15	Collecting Sect. 15 horses remaining.	
" 19.10.15	Collecting Sect. 8 horses admitted. 3 horses remaining.	
" 20.10.15	Collecting Sect. 24 horses admitted. 1 horse received and 1 horse discharged. 37 horses remaining. No. S.E. 833 Pte. Jones.S.A. returned from leave.	
" 21.10.15	Collecting Sect. 8 horses admitted. 3 horses no. remaining.	
" 22.10.15	42 horses remaining. Collecting Sect. 1 horse admitted. 1 horse arrived and marched to Poperinghe & remainder 35 sick for Advanced Veterinary Hospital. 10 horses remaining	

Army Form C. 2118.

WAR DIARY
or of No. F1 Mobile Veterinary Section
3rd Division
INTELLIGENCE SUMMARY.
(Erase heading not required.) No. 3.

Instructions regarding War Diaries and Intelligence Summaries are contained in F.S. Regs., Part II. and the Staff Manual respectively. Title pages will be prepared in manuscript.

by E. Lunedf. Capt.
O.C. F.M.V.S.

Hour, Date, Place	Summary of Events and Information	Remarks and references to Appendices
Poperinghe 23/10/15	Collecting Post. 10 horses remaining. Pte. PETTITT, J. admitted to hospital & returned to duty. No. S.E. No 687	
Steenvoorde 24/10/15	Section marched from Poperinghe, & took over next relief from No. 29 M.V.S. at STEENVOORDE. 3 horses left with No. 29 M.V.S. 1 horse taken over from No. 29 M.V.S. 17th Division. 8 horses remaining.	
" 25/10/15	Collecting Post. 8 remaining.	
" 26/10/15	Collecting Post. 1 horse admitted. 9 horses remaining	
" 27/10/15	Collecting Post. 9 horses admitted. 2 returned cured. 11 horses remaining. 2 N.C.O's & 6 Men joined No. F1 M.V.S. from No. 2 Vety. Hospital.	
" 28/10/15	Collecting Post. 17 horses admitted. 25 horses remaining	
" 29/10/15	Collecting Post. 3 horses admitted. 1 S Cox. & 6 Men evacuated to attached Veterinary Hospital. 2 N.C.O's & 9 men transferred from No. F1 to No. 2 Veterinary Hospital. Relief supplied by A.D.V.S. 2nd Army	
" 30/10/15	Collecting Post. 5 horses admitted. 13 horses remaining	
" 31/10/15	Collecting Post. 2 horses admitted. 17 horses remaining	

2nd 5

2nd Division

N° 3. Mtd. Vet. Sec.
Oct 1900
Vol XIV

121/7730
ans

WAR DIARY
or
INTELLIGENCE SUMMARY.

(Erase heading not required.)

W.3. M.V.S.

Army Form C. 2118.

Hour, Date, Place	Summary of Events and Information	Remarks and references to Appendices
3/10/15	Routine work. Inspects Div train horses.	
4	Casualties 47 horses to Base.	
5	Routine work. Inspects horses mustang ahead casualties 9 horses to Base.	
6	Routine work.	
7	Routine work. Casualties 5 " 1 mule.	
8	Routine work. Inspects Div team horses.	
	Routine work. Hauling Rifle Inspects	
9	Also helium, casualties 16 horses 3 mules.	
10	Routine work. Inspects [?]	
11	Routine work. Visits Div train horses.	
12	Routine work. Inspects	
13	Visits [?] Form Co. lives. Hauling [?] [?] veterinary hospitals week.	

Army Form C. 2118.

WAR DIARY
or
INTELLIGENCE SUMMARY.
(Erase heading not required.)

Instructions regarding War Diaries and Intelligence Summaries are contained in F. S. Regs., Part II. and the Staff Manual respectively. Title pages will be prepared in manuscript.

Hour, Date, Place	Summary of Events and Information	Remarks and references to Appendices
12-10-15	Routine work. Visited 3rd Div. train line. Evacuated 11 horses	
13-10-15	" Inspection M.C. Evacuated 8 horses	
14-10-15	Routine work. Evacuated 6 horses. Visited Div. train line	
15-10-15	Routine work.	
16-10-15	Routine work. Inspection Rifle Sangers. Visited train line	
17-10-15	" Evacuated 23 horses	
18-10-15	" Changed location of Section	
19-10-15	" Standing Fast. Evacuated 11 horses	
20-10-15	Routine work. Visited Div. train line	
21-10-15	" Evacuated 16 horses	
22-10-15	" Visited Div. train line	
23-10-15		

Army Form C. 2118.

WAR DIARY
or
INTELLIGENCE SUMMARY.
(Erase heading not required.)

Instructions regarding War Diaries and Intelligence Summaries are contained in F. S. Regs., Part II. and the Staff Manual respectively. Title pages will be prepared in manuscript.

Hour, Date, Place	Summary of Events and Information	Remarks and references to Appendices
24 - 10 - 15	Routine work. Rowalpindi 6 Horse	
25 - 10 - 15	" " Views Div. storeline	
26 - 10 - 15	" " Inspectors Rifles etc	
27 - 10 - 15	" " Rowalpindi 167 Horse	
28 - 10 - 15	" " Visits Div Storeline	
29 - 10 - 15	" " Rowalpindi 6 Horse	
	W. H. Jones 1st Bengal Lancers	
	A.D.V.S. leaves. Col.	
	Heyworth from Col. Verlin guard over 2	
30 - 10 - 15	Routenworth Verlin Cavalry	
	takes up charge	
	Routine work.	
31 - 10 - 15	" " Rowalpindi 7 Horse	
1 - 11 - 15	" " " "	
2 - 11 - 15	Inspection of Rifles etc	

WAR DIARY
INTELLIGENCE SUMMARY
(Erase heading not required.)

Army Form C. 2118.

Instructions regarding War Diaries and Intelligence Summaries are contained in F. S. Regs., Part II. and the Staff Manual respectively. Title pages will be prepared in manuscript.

Hour, Date, Place	Summary of Events and Information	Remarks and references to Appendices
3 – 11 – 15	Routine work:- Railway Rifle Wilwerwehr:	
4 – 11 – 15	" " Wheels 8 hrs	
5 – 11 – 15	" " Cupola Dia mtr charge	
6 – 11 – 15	" " Wheels 7 hrs	
7 – 11 – 15	" " Horn June	
8 – 11 – 15	" " Wheels 10 hrs	
9 – 11 – 15	" " " 12 hrs	
10 – 11 – 15	" " " 10 hrs	
11 – 11 – 15	" " " 12 hrs	
12 – 11 – 15	" " " 2 hrs Domette	
13 – 11 – 15	" " Repairs all lines mtr charge	
	Wheels 17 hrs Depression	
14 – 11 – 15	Rifle Artillery & Sheary	
	Routine work Auditing new line for line	
	Wire treatment Wheels 3 hrs	
16 – 11 – 15	Routine work Wheels 7 hrs	

Army Form C. 2118.

WAR DIARY
or
INTELLIGENCE SUMMARY.
(Erase heading not required.)

Instructions regarding War Diaries and Intelligence Summaries are contained in F. S. Regs., Part II. and the Staff Manual respectively. Title pages will be prepared in manuscript.

Hour, Date, Place	Summary of Events and Information	Remarks and references to Appendices
17-11-15	Rotine work. wounded 21 hores	
18-11-15	" 3 hores	
19-11-15	Various lines under change. wounded 8 hores	
20-11-15	Routine work.	
21-11-15	Routine work. Inspection of Rifles & billets by Sgt Collin - Corpl Carroll & Gr Gallop reports not to h no 10/105 Camp Sumpter. Gr. not [illegible] wounded	
22-11-15	Manoeuvres to no 10 / ch (ref) wounded Hores. Routine work. wounded 10 hores	
23-11-15	Speaks all hores now under charge wounded 10 hores	
24-11-15	Routine work.	
25-11-15	Inspection Saddlery Rifle	
26-11-15	Routine work. wounded 8 hores	

Army Form C. 2118.

WAR DIARY
or
INTELLIGENCE SUMMARY.
(Erase heading not required.)

W.B.N.S.

Instructions regarding War Diaries and Intelligence Summaries are contained in F.S. Regs., Part II. and the Staff Manual respectively. Title pages will be prepared in manuscript.

Hour, Date, Place	Summary of Events and Information	Remarks and references to Appendices
26-11-15	Routine work. Inlieu of line trenches reviewing lines are charge. Gunpickets tiffs and sentries lines.	WNSR
27-11-15	Routine work. Movement to first line	WNSR
28-11-15	"	WNSR
29-11-15	Church.	
30-11-15	Routine work. Strength 10 horses.	WNSR

(9 29 6) W 3332—1107 100,000 10/13 H W V Forms/C. 2118/10.

2ND DIVISION
DIVL. TROOPS

NO. 3 MOBILE VETERINARY SECT
DEC 1915 - DEC 1916.

Constantine
MacBrany
of
E.B.
M.V.G.
Ivy Dix
From Dec 1st 1915 to Apl 3rd 1916

Nov 15
9
8
7
-
9

WAR DIARY
or
INTELLIGENCE SUMMARY

Army Form C. 2118.

B h V S 2nd Div

Place	Date	Hour	Summary of Events and Information	Remarks and references to Appendices
Bethune	1/2/15		Routine work R of Section. Inspected Rifles and Horses of No 2 ank fir 2nd Div. Train. Movements 3 horses listed.	A/F 93
"	2/2/15		Routine work. Hauling slag for horse standings. Visits to Dir C train — no movements 7 horses	A/F 93
"	3/2/15		Routine work. Inspected Saddlery Issues	A/F 93
"	4/2/15		Routine work. Movements 8 horses. Visit to Wee of ASC	A/F 93
"	5/2/15		Routine work " " 3 " Inspected horses of MT Co, train	A/F 93
"	6/2/15		Inspection of Rifles and Saddlery. Routine work. Movements 6 horses.	A/F 93
"	7/2/15		Routine work. Inspected Rifles and Horses of No 1 Div Train. Movements 13 horses.	A/F 93
"	8/2/15		Routine work. Exercise nose individually. No sick p h	A/F 93
"	9/2/15		Routine work. Movements 8 horses	A/F 93
"	10/2/15		" " 11 horses and Inspected horses of Bontpay	A/F 93
"	11/2/15		Train and T R h Unit in myshauge Routine work. Inspection of Standin & Iron Ration	A/F 93

Army Form C. 2118.

WAR DIARY
or
INTELLIGENCE SUMMARY.
(Erase heading not required.)

N° 3 R. V. S. 2nd Div

Instructions regarding War Diaries and Intelligence Summaries are contained in F. S. Regs., Part II. and the Staff Manual respectively. Title pages will be prepared in manuscript.

Place	Date	Hour	Summary of Events and Information	Remarks and references to Appendices
Bethune	Dec. 15 12		Routine work. Grapeels lines N° 3 C. tram and tramends	W8302
			13 lines Repr.	W8301
"	13th		Routine work.	W8302
"	14th		" 15 tramends 12 lines and mapeels rifle and Pet.	W8302
"	15th		" " mapeels 14 Div Co tram lines	W8302
"	16th		" " tramends 12 lines and mapeels lines 7	W8302
			Midnight tram	
"	17th		Routine work, tramends 6 lines	W8302
"	18th		" "	W8303
"	19th		" 27 " Grapeels 1.5.2 Coy lines	W8302
"	20th		" " Grapeels and tramends	W8302
"	21st		" " tramends 62 lines. Grapeels wet ri' lines	W8302
"	22nd		" " 8 lines.	W8300
"	23rd		" Grapeels lines of Morty tram and N° 3 C.	W8302
"	24th		" " of M.V.S. and eastery	W8302
"	25th		" " of 14 Div tram and rifle	W8302

T2134. Wt. W708–776. 500000. 4/15. Sir J. C. & S.

WAR DIARY
or
INTELLIGENCE SUMMARY.
(Erase heading not required.)

Army Form C. 2118.

Place	Date	Hour	Summary of Events and Information	Remarks and references to Appendices
Bethune	Dec-15 26th		Routine work. Movements 14 horses.	AF6368 AF6368
"	27th		" Visits 2 w/o Caghier at Cheques and paid him	
"	28th		Inspection of horses of North Re. Train. Routine work. Movements 13 horses	AF6368 AF6368
"	29th		Routine work. Many movements & horses admitted to Surgery. Argyles breaking for 5 w.v.D.	
BUSNES	30th		Routine work. Argyles broke at Snepeels rifle	AF6368 AF6368
"	31st		Routine work and cleaning up after 33rd Dis w S Little Reserve and a host of despicable Journalier hospitality Tunnel	
"	Jan 1/16		ft. to train	
"	2nd		Routine work. Half holiday for men not in Duty. Movements 14 horses. Train Cies aferred	AF6368 AF6368
"	3rd		" " Visits 33 Ds. Dis town its Qm. Loose Box-line Horsemans to other lines working 2/1/16a Routine work	AF6368 AF6368
"	4th		" Inspects W3 Co Horses at Le Hameau	AF6368 AF6368
			W.t.C. — and my Cs. and Bulles	

WAR DIARY
INTELLIGENCE SUMMARY

Army Form C. 2118.

(Erase heading not required.)

No 3 M.V.S. 2nd Div

Instructions regarding War Diaries and Intelligence Summaries are contained in F.S. Regs., Part II. and the Staff Manual respectively. Title pages will be prepared in manuscript.

Place	Date	Hour	Summary of Events and Information	Remarks and references to Appendices
	Jan-15.			
Berre	5.		Routine work. Imperial's 3 horse, Imperial's lines 1/5th	W98R
"	6.		" Imperial's Ambulance at Berre	W98R
			Routine work, Imperial's billets and secured two very large sheds for horse standing corps growing heavily	W98R
"	7.		Routine work Imperials 2nd horse line	W98R
"	8.		" Imperials 8 horse. and Imperial's lines N3	W98R
"	9.		" train at Berre	W98R
			Routine work, Imperials	W98R
"	9.		" Visits No to C horse line.	W98R
"	10.		" Imperials 8 horse. Visits 1st Plt 33 Bn	W98R
"	11.		" train horse line — Imperial's hit C horse	W98R
"	12.		Routine work, Visits billets and 2nd horse line	W98R
"	13.		" Visits Lieutenant and N°3 & horse line	W98R
"	14.		" Imperial's mv.8 horse and sanitary.	W98R
"	15.		" Imperial's 5 horse and Imperial's h&2 and 4 Co.	W98R
"	16.		" Imperial's 8 2nd horse line and No 33rd mams	W98R

WAR DIARY
or
INTELLIGENCE SUMMARY

Army Form C. 2118.

Place	Date	Hour	Summary of Events and Information	Remarks and references to Appendices
	Jan 17th 16			
Busnes	17th		Routine work and preparation for move. Movements 1 horse.	W.B.96
Bethune	18th		Moves back to Bethune billets over from 12th Div. more.	W.B.96
			Took over for 2nd Div. to clean up.	
"	19th		Routine work. Withdrawing hauling day etc. & cleaning up. Movements rifts. Visits to Div. Com. at Annezin	W.B.96
"	20th		Routine work. Movements 21 horse and motorcycle horse & photo team.	W.B.96
"	21st		" 7 horse	W.B.96
"	22nd		" 16 horse. Motorcycle pickets and orderly	W.B.96
"	23rd		" 16 horse	W.B.96
"	24th		" Visits horse lines of No. 4 Co. at Hinges and No. 2 Co.	W.B.96
"	25th		" Movements 22 horse	W.B.96
"	26th		" 10 horse. Motorcycle horse ?	W.B.96
			Horse Artillery & No. 3 Co-joan	
"	27th		Routine work. Movements 16 horse & motorcycle belts	W.B.96
"	28th		" Visits horse lines No. 17 to 19th Co. Joan, and No. 2 Co. Motorcycle rifts.	W.B.96

WAR DIARY
or
~~INTELLIGENCE~~ SUMMARY.
(Erase heading not required.)

Army Form C. 2118.

N° 3 N.Y.S. 2nd Div.

Place	Date	Hour	Summary of Events and Information	Remarks and references to Appendices
Bethune	Jan 29th		Routine work. Arrivals 16 horses	AF.C.2118.
"	30th		" 20 horses. Arrivals not to have	AF.C.2118.
"	31st		Visits Artillery Pourt. Arrivals all horses	AF.C.2118.
"	Feb 1st		9/2nd Div train Routine work. Arrivals 40 horses mostly for other Divs. Arrivals rifles & billets	AF.C.2118.
"	2nd		Routine work. Arrivals 13 horses. Arrivals N°2 and 3 Co train	AF.C.2118.
"	3rd		" Arrivals horse N°6 Coy train and see N Reuz	AF.C.2118.
"	4th		Calls att to 2nd Div train	AF.C.2118.
"	5th		Routine work. Arrivals 17 horses	AF.C.2118.
"	6th		" 3 horses. Arrivals horse Coy of 16	AF.C.2118.
"	7th		Oh to train and not to Civil clinic Routine work Arrivals 15 horses	AF.C.2118.
"	8th		" Arrivals horse & horse surgery Arrivals 27 horses	AF.C.2118.
"	9th		" Arrivals N°3 Co train horse	AF.C.2118.

WAR DIARY
INTELLIGENCE SUMMARY. W3 h Y 8

Army Form C. 2118.

Place	Date	Hour	Summary of Events and Information	Remarks and references to Appendices
Bethune	Apl-16 10th		Proceeded to England on leave returned to Boulogne	W3P8R
"	11th		Journey to 24 hours Returned	W3B95
"	12th		"	W3B95
"	13th		" 10 hrs recruits	W3B95
"	14th		"	W3B95
"	15th		" 22 "	W3B95
"	16th		"	W3B95
"	17th		" "	W3B95
"	18th		Moved back to Chorue. Armis Back Windsor from hill to clear up after 12th Div. Cartin work	W3P8R
"	19th		Cleaning up	W3B95
"	20th		Visits Nos 2 and 3 Co 2nd Div train	W3B95
"	21st		" Movements 12 hrs	W3B95
"	22nd		" Inspects whole section as Nos 1 & 2 tram hers	W3B95
"	23rd		" Movements 8 hrs	W3B95

Army Form C. 2118.

WAR DIARY
or
INTELLIGENCE SUMMARY.
(Erase heading not required.)

1st 3 M.V.S. 2nd Div

Place	Date	Hour	Summary of Events and Information	Remarks and references to Appendices
Busnes	Feb 16			
	24th		Routine work. Impreats w/s & Shiers. Visits to Ht F & howrs	WD30?
"	25th		"	WD30?
"	26th		— Twaenats 14 horses. Impreats w/s & town	WD30?
"	27th			WD20?
Bethune	28th		Preparing to move. Moved to Bethune 10 hours to Bethune.	WD20? WD20?
"	29th			WD20?
Barlin	March 1st		Routine work and cleaning up. Spent all for H.S but Rive trip to hind. Thrice have stable frame.	
			it but no horse. Proceed sheets for left Co horses also m a few days hard with the winter in cold Yper	
			for A.M.V.S. Newport. All the time taken up for	
			A.D.V.S. Nice about to remain here	
			but	
"	2nd		Routine work. Always up. Withdrawing and landing flap Twaents 8 horses	WD20? WD20?
"	3rd		Routine work, and clean up. Impreats all horses two	WD20?

Army Form C. 2118.

WAR DIARY
or
INTELLIGENCE SUMMARY.
(Erase heading not required.)

W.B. h. V.8. 2 w/

Instructions regarding War Diaries and Intelligence Summaries are contained in F. S. Regs., Part II. and the Staff Manual respectively. Title pages will be prepared in manuscript.

Place	Date	Hour	Summary of Events and Information	Remarks and references to Appendices
	March -16			
Babu	4R		Routine work. Inspection.	W.B.B.R
"	5R		" Rifle Inspection. Res. Pmk. and Coke reports for Duty.	W.B.h.R
"	6R		" Inveralis 13 hrs. Inspection hrs 2 Coys.	W.B.B
"	7R		Drills Drof. Coys 27th Sh Cav.	W.B.B
"	8R		Routine work. Inspection Farriers & Saddlers.	W.B.B
"	9R		"	W.B.B
				W.B.B
"	10R		Inst R Service rolls and gun cavalry Tree	W.B.B
"	11R		Routine work. Inveralis 10 hrs.	W.B.B
"	12R		" Inspection lines 27th Sh Cav	W.B.B
"	13R		" Inspection M.T./T/8.	W.B.B
			Pte Stewart Marks for Duty and Pte	
			Walker Transferred to Indian View Hospital	
"	14R		Routine work. Inveralis 11 hrs.	W.B.B
"	15R		Routine work. Inspects 2 Cos lines.	W.B.B
"	16R		" Inveralis 17 hrs. Inspection relief.	W.B.B

T.J.134. Wt. W708—776. 500000. 4/15. Sir J.C. & S.

WAR DIARY
INTELLIGENCE SUMMARY

Army Form C. 2118.

Place	Date	Hour	Summary of Events and Information	Remarks and references to Appendices
Barlin	Mar-16 17th		Routine work. Coy School. Inspection Nº 4 Co hoses	AF C.2118
"	18th		"	AF C.2118
"	19th		Inspection Nº 2 & 3 Coy horses	AF C.2118
"	20th		Inspection of Mr. 8 horses + Battery	AF C.2118
"	21st		Inoculation 20 horses. Preparations for hike	AF C.2118
Bruay	22nd		hiked to Bruay. Cleaning up. Ans cavalry stay in horse stands up	AF C.2118
"	23rd		Routine work. Inspection Nº 1 Co at Bruer, and Nº 2 Nº at Le Rinelette	AF C.2118
"	24th		Routine work. Building horse lines and covering in Stables and Sentry. Increase 15 horses	AF C.2118
"	25th		Visits Nº 2 and Nº 3 Co. Sick Draw. Inspecting N.Rifle and Saddlery	AF C.2118
"	26th		Routine work. Inspection of Mr. 8 horses and kit	AF C.2118
"	27th		Co train with Ms Ohms train Routine work. Officers averages 51 h51 of C by 9 C/n for Evry. Caught Smith (coy) 6 horse in Clothing + Kees	AF C.2118

WAR DIARY
or
INTELLIGENCE SUMMARY.
(Erase heading not required.)

Army Form C. 2118.

Place	Date	Hour	Summary of Events and Information	Remarks and references to Appendices
Bruay	Mch-16 28th		Routine work. Inspection N°3 and 1st & N°4 Coy 2nd Dn from Inspection 19 horses	WRR6?
"	29th		" Pte Douglas joined	WRR6?
"	30th		6 days pay in absence without leave for 3 horses	WRR6?
"	31st		Routine work. Rifle Inspection. 1st West Proceeds to 15 Blaris on leave	WRR6?
"	Apl 1st		Routine work. Inspection Horses. Inspection of Saddlery	WRR6?
"	2nd		" Inspection 16 horses	WRR6?
"	3rd		" Inspection of Saddlery. Includes and DeRn Returns	WRR6?
"	4th		" Inspection of Mn S horses. Coy School	WRR6?
"	5th		" Valis work as WR? to team has sim field	WRR6?
"	6th		" Inspection 16 horses.	WRR6?
"	7th		" Pte Potts proceeds to England on leave. Inspection horses. Lt DH Lo Train. Valis WR? S Major Dolton WR? S proceeds to Elen on return. Yhee. 3rd rt. Lucarne the Mrs sections WR? S	WRR6?
"	8th		Routine work. Inspection 8 horses. Valis WR? S Mes	WRR6?

Army Form C. 2118.

WAR DIARY
or
INTELLIGENCE SUMMARY.
(Erase heading not required.)

Instructions regarding War Diaries and Intelligence Summaries are contained in F.S. Regs., Part II. and the Staff Manual respectively. Title pages will be prepared in manuscript.

Place	Date	Hour	Summary of Events and Information	Remarks and references to Appendices
Sonnay	Apl 9th		Routine work of section. Visits A.D.r.S. Nice. Ypres lines to lines.	W.P.26?
"	10th		Routine work. Ypres lines 20 lines	A.D.r.S Nice
"	11th		Routine work. Rifle Ypres lines	A.D.r. S Nice
"	12th		Visits 1½ Ph G Qu 1. and Ypres lines Ju 3 Co.	A.D. S Nice
"	13th		Routine work. Rising School and Rifle Inst. A.D.r S. Nice	A.D.r.S Nice
"	14th		" Visits A.D.r S Nice	A.D.S Nice
"	15th		" " Ypres lines	A.D.S Nice
"	16th		" Battle lines Ypres lines. V.S. A.D.S Nice	A.D.S Nice
"	17th		" Visits A.D.r S Nice. Ypres lines Ju 3 Co lines	A.D.S Nice
"	18th		" Ypres lines 17 loss. Visits A.D.r S Nice	A.D.S Nice
"	19th		" A.D.r. S Nice. Plu rath reports for July	A.D.S Nice
Berlin	19th		Went to Berlin.	
"	20th		Routine work and cleaning up. Rifle Ypres lines. Rifle Ypres Ku W.P.26	
"	21st		" Visits Nice of A.D.r S at Saint Michelle	W.P.26?
			Ypres lines Ypres Ju 3 lines Pn le oran	

T2134. Wt. W708-776. 500000. 4/15. Sir J. C. & S.

WAR DIARY
or
INTELLIGENCE SUMMARY.   W.B. N.Z. & ...

Army Form C. 2118.

Place	Date	Hour	Summary of Events and Information	Remarks and references to Appendices
Berlin	Apl -16 22nd		Routine work. Visits Offr & N.C.O's. Sgt Holden of... Section and Pte. Doyle of the Sect. both has at R&B... Re being struck off strength of Section Trades S...	
			& & Sgt Holden awarded 2/3 days No 1 FP	AR2767
	23rd		Routine work. Bomb School visits Offr & Other - Inspects	AR2767
			of Retaliation and Rifles	
	24th		Trenches 3) hrs. Visits Offr S. Offer	AR2767
	25th		- Inspects Itd. gli. and N.o g. Ca lines ARS. Offer	AR2767
	26th		- Trenches 2½ hrs. Offr. S. Offer Inspects	AR2767
			Offrs and N.C.O's lines.	
	27th		Routine work. Visits Offer. S. Offer. Inspects N.3/B.4 lines	AR2767
	28th		"	AR2767
			16 Ph.G. lines	
	29th		Trenches 1½ hrs. Offr. S. Offer.	AR2767
	30th		- Visits Offr. S. Offer and Over H.O Offer	AR2767
			Inspects lines from - Lastly Rd Rfls	
			Visits 12th transport lines and remounts lines	AR2767

CONFIDENTIAL.

WAR DIARY.
OF

No. 3. Australian Veterinary Section
2nd Div.

FROM May 1st -16   To May 31st -16.

WAR DIARY
or
INTELLIGENCE SUMMARY

Army Form C. 2118.

(Erase heading not required.)

Instructions regarding War Diaries and Intelligence Summaries are contained in F.S. Regs., Part II. and the Staff Manual respectively. Title pages will be prepared in manuscript.

Place	Date	Hour	Summary of Events and Information	Remarks and references to Appendices
Berlin	May -16 1st		Routine work. Early morning & before and during several views of one. Train attaining Imperials speed of 115 Ph and no 2. to train	AP&62
"	2nd		Continued. Imperials 67 feet – by no. Wacerele's	AP&62
"	3rd		It loose. Various views of A.W. & Routine work. Rising before. Rly inspection.	AP&62
"	4th		Alice and inspection of 2nd Panel La Lune	AP&62
"	5th		Railways. A.W. S. view Pi Shinav E Gear Movements 23 line Imperials Area 1/2	AP&62
			It and 2 Co train A.W. S. view Vials 23 & Jumelling Co Lepy	
"	6th		Routine work. Rising before A.O.C. Office. Imperial 5 to train and 3 O. Constantin. Return Lt Gnr Section	AP&62
"	7th		Routine work of section. Imperials 120 Phy Obs Blue Varies Alice of Awg & Alleleles A.O.C. 47 & 48 & 3 Div – on way to Div 6 conference called by Brig S. 1st Army	AP&62

WAR DIARY
or
INTELLIGENCE SUMMARY.

Army Form C. 2118.

Place	Date	Hour	Summary of Events and Information	Remarks and references to Appendices
Berlin	May.16 8.		Routine work. Riding School and Gunners Inspection of Battery & Harness Mg. S. Venite 120. Bty. Horse Lines. Adv. 2 & Vhee and Mr. Sre. Sg.	WPBR
"	9th		Routine work. Rev.w Zelgul. Radio Show of Adv 2. and Corps Cashier at Regrener. Buss on Section. Horsewals 21 hors.	WPBR
"	10t		Routine work. Riding School & Gunners. Radio Adv. S. Vhee Iss Mr. Sre Gusst G and 12.5 H Heavy Bty IS NA Bonf Stf. Denlyp reports for Duty van Luck	WPBR
"	11th		Routine work. Gunpowd. Inspection As Mr. C Capt. Gryth special to new ASC S. 2nd Dis. Visits Vhee Adv. S. 12 or N Bty 1. 23 3 Summler. Co Horses Mr. Gryth Mrs Mr 6th 2 who form and Jovenes Ce for Mr. Sandists to the billet at Samu in Sheets	WPBR
"	12th		Cline work. Riding School Preparing for here at-Day Inspection Hors 7 to Mr L. 9 - Dine Domin	WPBR

WAR DIARY
or
INTELLIGENCE SUMMARY.

Army Form C. 2118.

Place	Date	Hour	Summary of Events and Information	Remarks and references to Appendices
Berlin	May 1-16			
	13th		Change location to Conway to Ronnoyeur S.S.D.W. with detachment to Glimy Ambulance to same place for Sect. all here to date.	WD36R
	14th		Routine work musketry lecture. Inspection and inoculation of 99th Regt. by 9 Lts & M.O. to new arrivals. Selects distribution of 99th I.B. transport and Tunnel of records.	WD36R
	15th		Routine work. Rouge School. Visits by Philip Front and Generals Horse of Mo2 and 7th Div. Les Drews. Les interview with Co Comte de Donn.	WD36R
	16th		Received 13 horses including charge of 2 Lt Col Bridge 19th Div. Routine work. Building Dumps for training to Lt Col prepares trees of Lts of Co trains 1 Sec 13 hours 2 Yorks 99th & 98 Inf Corps Chai Sect. 1 since to M.V.S. Visits by Gen Monto V0% Dire? and Conjunts.	WD36R

WAR DIARY or INTELLIGENCE SUMMARY

Army Form C. 2118.

Place	Date	Hour	Summary of Events and Information	Remarks and references to Appendices
Bruay	May 16		Routine work. Rising below wire June 28. Visits by AD.V.S. Inspects mules & horses of Gros D.A.D at the V.S/C Visits V.S/C at Bruay.	
"	17.		Routine work. Rising below Whistler AW lame horse & injured back and hirds. Not severe. Slipped 5 mules 999[2] Sqn h.Q late 8. Visits Berlin and Capt Brown ar 2 ans Inspects horses & train horses Received 23 horses for reserve transferred unit of Div. Visits by A.D.V.S. Present 15 16 horses.	ADVS
"	18th		Routine work and Ro in police. Inspects Rifles Visits Rifle Point Conroy and inspects horses of Gron arranged will Col Conroy for transport and want part. Inspection for horses to artillery Sent 19 horses & Gro D.A.D. for reserve General Shaw tot 100 & fild Ambulance visits M.G. and lives their horses No injuries Horses here fell or lame horse or lure Apple here	ADVS
	19d			ADVS

WAR DIARY
or
INTELLIGENCE SUMMARY.
(Erase heading not required.)

Army Form C. 2118.

Place	Date	Hour	Summary of Events and Information	Remarks and references to Appendices
Bruay	May 1-16			
	20th		Relieved 5th Dn Co. Brown by rpairs. Hauling Rubble. Sent Dump Cart & 1 Plympt Hauling Rubble. Visited the Dn Co - took Major Grieves & Col Booth C/O 2nd Div down to start in the clearing & loading for the Divl Dump. Inspected No 2 Co lines and attended Coy Lines Inspn. Left lulies to be relieved by Dunkerque Millicles horse Steam lee. by Dunkerque from Le Conté. On line made 4 m. traversed 11 lines. Visits until 1/2 o/c.	WRBR
	21st		On C/Pe 115 Dn Co. down hot de Ganches with No 3 Co. Damping line to them. Dn. Ho trellis. Sent to Gromches to pass & inspect Canoy & clocks and Dumpeart Wheel. seen Mr Gloss Continued to Completion delivery of Imps. Sectio Charge Sent to Le Conté for change of Gn. Weld. Reserve orrs to be in readiness at ordinary hos (visits sub to relieve at Rebreuve. Visits left to lines and see No 2 W. C.	
	22nd		Sace left lulines by N.T.B. Pte Thomas sunts F. Hosp. 105th F. Amb.	WR61

WAR DIARY
INTELLIGENCE SUMMARY

Army Form C. 2118.

Place	Date	Hour	Summary of Events and Information	Remarks and references to Appendices
Bruay	May-16			
	22nd		Returned & enquiry a.m. Visits down to HQs and Rifle Butt. All coy transport inspected. Able to dine at Dinner. Pte Doyle reported by Sergt Weston found drunk at Allouette and was sent to HQ13 Battery HQ. Pte Liddle warned for 2 Vol Rest Zuytpeene. Votes N°3 Co train House wood Open Ment - Arleux - Johays Native Work Rosey School. Visited Rifling Range. Parents section of MG/Bosches inspection half way to Houchin Pl. Engl'd Sketches N°2 Note Spare with Lecture in course. Radio Insh Inspection 9-30 for the wounding of Sergt Morales OC no. 8 Pl Hughes attended Hº.	
	23rd		Lucas Imperials Rifles Awards to 11.0 hr Cpl Greenmore 1st Pte Smiley 2nd Cottrell's Lancaster Dinn and 3rd Bardette by Bandmaster Rhind gave Cheers to Seargent-Major and per 4th Pl Reserve Imperials all less of Gdsn foot-market Touch	
	25th			

Army Form C. 2118.

WAR DIARY
or
INTELLIGENCE SUMMARY
(Erase heading not required.)

Instructions regarding War Diaries and Intelligence Summaries are contained in F.S. Regs., Part II. and the Staff Manual respectively. Title pages will be prepared in manuscript.

Place	Date	Hour	Summary of Events and Information	Remarks and references to Appendices
BRUAY	May 16 26th 27th		Visits Kannoon & met ADS & the Maj. Gen. at 7.30am for statement to take every possible action in hospital about 11 a.m. and found a very suitable location for HQ. Several hours spent in reconnaissance to learn WB. Up to now roads which ought to have been changed before they got so bad, launched in the possibility of course the visits to Bruay & recles in the bus. Purchase of pigs, 10x½ & ADMS conf with our & pth charge of 124, 107 Fld, 42nd ADMS conf Bulls up courses for men and clearing up generally. Evacuates 17 Purbs & mules, for 4th Div	A.D.M.S.R
FRESNEBURY	28th		Cases holings and trips. Reviews Diwath charge of 14th Corps Fd Ms Dis. at Rebreuve.	A.D.M.S.R
"	29th		Visits all cos & one train.	
"	30th		Review conf. Receives infection specify travels & much rain through might which stocks from in their lutts.	

T2131. Wt. W708—773. 500000. 4/16. Sir J.C.&S.

Army Form C. 2118.

WAR DIARY
or
INTELLIGENCE SUMMARY.
(Erase heading not required.)

Instructions regarding War Diaries and Intelligence Summaries are contained in F. S. Regs., Part II. and the Staff Manual respectively. Title pages will be prepared in manuscript.

Place	Date	Hour	Summary of Events and Information	Remarks and references to Appendices
	May -16			
FRESNICOURT	30.		Visits he fore 5 [Div] Train. Caught Divnl Generals conv. Inf. Coy. Lived improved. Routine Work.	
"	31.		Evacuated 14 horses : 3 mules h/m Conval - withdrawl b Res of Benedictn (Sup) Violin hos 2/3. Section 2 w/ Res D/S and 72 ft Hvy Bty transf from Reserve 1st Ry railways	OPB?

T/134. Wt. W708-776. 500000. 4/15. Sir J. C. & S.

CONFIDENTIAL

War Diary

of

No. 3. 7th. V.S. 2nd Div.

From June 1st–16 to June 30th–16

WAR DIARY
or
INTELLIGENCE SUMMARY.

Army Form C. 2118.

Place	Date	Hour	Summary of Events and Information	Remarks and references to Appendices
Froment	June 1	10.-	Routine work of section. Rosney Relieved. Visits to HQ of 1/No. and reserves. New hut completed for R.F.C. Polyclinic erected.	ARFA1
"	2nd		Routine & ordinary work. Relieved Visits all to R.E.S. farm and 2nd 1st Div. Slanneret Supply & who was in front of Army in Flandres. Visits Rue 161 the Lieut Helling night R.F.C. visits until yesterday lines and wounded enclosed MC	ARFA2
"	3rd		Routine work. Visits lines of Div farm and Div 1 & Altham to La Here	ARFA3
"	4th– 5th		Routine work. Inspected lines of No 2 and 4 to farm Routine work and ordinary scheme meeting multiple. Inspected Arrree 1 16 Div CCS HQ to farm	ARFA4
"	6th		Routine work. Rosney Supdent Army sent show has visits to Corps 14 to No 2nd Reserve BHR and 12 Gr by Dr Loy me	ARFA5
"	7th		Routine work. Vaccinates 90 horses mule mostly to Air Dis Allies Horre by Ambulance stamps	ARFA6

WAR DIARY
or
INTELLIGENCE SUMMARY.
(Erase heading not required.)

Army Form C. 2118.

Place	Date	Hour	Summary of Events and Information	Remarks and references to Appendices
Havrincourt	June 7th		Routine work. Visits 129 Bty. Horselines and wagon lines. Rode train. Rode to Blowurbers Rambam "Willi" Capeels Destroy gun N° Fecilis.	
"	9th		Routine work. Rode to Meu Maison & Foulzee. W. of Y.Gin. All our forward arcs very distinct. Went into place. N.g. and of-in weather. Rode George swallowed. Follows by Nort and brings Shires 147 ? On Road rode to the horse lines in the area. The 116 the and the place. Visits all C.o's of Guns. For am. Routine work. Traverete Dg aimed. Sunny Jan all day.	aC30? aC30? aC30?
"	15th		Visits Mer of N.C.P. Returned, feeels Sick Arrived Goran. 129 Bty Horse Lines Be Good things from General Reeves So horse answer 3 much Society B. Three Questo. Wesk Major Hothly in hange of Divenue Vet-	aC30? aC30? aC30?
"	11th			

Army Form C. 2118.

WAR DIARY
or
INTELLIGENCE SUMMARY
(Erase heading not required.)

Instructions regarding War Diaries and Intelligence Summaries are contained in F. S. Regs., Part II. and the Staff Manual respectively. Title pages will be prepared in manuscript.

Place	Date	Hour	Summary of Events and Information	Remarks and references to Appendices
Fleurbaix	9 June 16 – 12th		Routine work. Brig School Visits to Company Hd Qrs Horse lines of 2nd Reserve Bth and all Lgt. 2nd Bn. teams sent to RHS 3 lines of 15 Pr Co train Running. Visits from 2y transport lines and sausage Balloon with man. – Shrapnel.	DR96P
"	13th		Routine work. Received 27 horses mules, melachines 13, Horses, mules, Lubechs horses by float. Chaplain Clayton Burns from Mohuse. Visits ful Lachin and Pere return to MC. Visits Reserve Bth and tea on horse return to MC. by float.	AWG AWG6 AWG6P
"	14th 15th		Routine work. Visited 2nd Bn from Coy Sgts. Conclm. Routine work. Inspected Rifles and Scabbard.	AWG6 AWG6P
"	16th		Routine work. Visits Gnr Reserve Pit and went to form Arrived 13 horses and 2 mules. Strag. 85	AWG6
"	17th		Routine work. Visits by DOW VS ? Aus PN Div. Rev. Le Condier & Allie	AWG6P

T2134. Wt. W708—776. 500000. 4/15. Sir J. C. & S.

WAR DIARY
or
INTELLIGENCE SUMMARY
(Erase heading not required.)

Army Form C. 2118.

Place	Date	Hour	Summary of Events and Information	Remarks and references to Appendices
Kromeroid	June 18th		Routine work. Visits both and to Olr Co train. Hd Pry Staffar out in Wh. N.S. M.O. Mr. Qur Co. Visits No 3 & to Rly R.H.Dn and Reservals. Two cars.	WRP&R
"	19th		Routine work. Visits by R.O. & R.h.Dn. Performer transport FHQ2. V.Hosp & out. Hd on leave leotn Man. of R&PR	WRP&R
			Morning. Inspects all horses of R & Pk until arr. of train	
	20th		Leave slopper for myself only. Routine work. Ple Itala forecasts. Leave warrants 17 cars	WRP&R
	21st		Routine work. Inspects Hd. Qrs and Hd. Co. train and inspects Hd. Qrs. & Hd annual of R to Reserve R. Painting wagons. Visits Hd 3 Co train. Ple Makrill Thoma War Dental Hosp. Leave again	WRP&R
			shipped 2 but words promis silence. he 27th not adusere enquiry.	
	22nd		Routine work. Ryle Inspector. Inspects Hup here 6.40 & 1.60 train. Hosp. train. Constreting Ready Kalmek Mullarn by Pk	WRP&R

WAR DIARY
INTELLIGENCE SUMMARY

Army Form C. 2118.

Place	Date	Hour	Summary of Events and Information	Remarks and references to Appendices
FRESNICOURT	June-16 23rd		Routine work and Musketry School. Visits 2 to Reg. P.C. Lecture on the pen. rifle and magazine. Pte Smile returns from leave. Lieut. West P.H. & Force Sis	
"	24th		Routine work. Musketry 23 hours 52 min. Enlisted. Major WBCS turns in report. Musketry	WRBR
"	25th		Visits to OM Company & Co train, 1st & 2nd Rg Pic	WRBR
"	26th		Routine work. Visits No 3 Coy train	WRBR
"	26th 9/6/"		Routine work. Visits 2nd Reg P.C. Musketry. Visits later & Musketry fields and him. Its Oc and Lt S.C. A complete Inspection. Its OM C Lyttead-	WRBR
"	27th		2nd Rye train Musketry B Chose Village End Rule Routine work. Enlisted Feb Rachie & Mensur and Jean	WRBR
"	28th		Routine work. Company Commandos on leave K Ryland. Pte Spence proceeds on leave to Rome Pie and sent to W.S. case of Sawmills. Visits to Mo. No. 4 and No. 2 Coy train. Received Conveyance x	WRBR

Instructions regarding War Diaries and Intelligence Summaries are contained in F. S. Regs., Part II. and the Staff Manual respectively. Title pages will be prepared in manuscript.

WAR DIARY
or
~~INTELLIGENCE SUMMARY.~~
(Erase heading not required.)

Army Form C. 2118.

Place	Date	Hour	Summary of Events and Information	Remarks and references to Appendices
	June 1916.			
FRESNICOURT	28th		of Drugs for re-issue to various Units of 2nd Div. Painting Ambulance. Received several Surplus horses for re-issue.	A.R.B.R.
"	29th		Routine work. Building Curbs behind horse Standings. Visited 2nd Res. Park and sent in horse to M.V.S.	A.R.B.R.
"	30th		Routine work. Sent 2 surplus horses to Remount Section Sommelieu. Evacuated 16 horses & 1 mule to Neufchatel. Conducting party returned 11.30 p.m. 29th. Visited HdQrs Co. No 4 and 3 Co 2nd Div. Train. New A.D.V.S. arrived today.	A.R.B.R.

T2134. Wt. W708–776. 500000. 4/15. Sir J. C. & S.

Vol 22

No 3 Mob. Vet. Section

CONFIDENTIAL.

WAR DIARY.

OF

1st B.M.G.S.

From July 1st -16
to July 31st -16.

WAR DIARY
~~INTELLIGENCE SUMMARY~~

Army Form C. 2118.

Place	Date	Hour	Summary of Events and Information	Remarks and references to Appendices
FRESNICOURT	July 1st		Routine work. Rugby School visits 2nd Bn Rif. Bde. H.Q. Div Co. 2nd Div. Ham outside Co team. Called at Place of Major Gurwood newly appointed ADMS 2nd Div. Rolf here at first time which we met 15th/r S Staffs. Places in slump in Thiévilliers and moved for Berlin to Beuvry. Remained in slump for night. Day and Maj visits hill hopes westward no R N Du Injects the Sector.	[signature]
"	2nd		Routine work. Inspection of Extempore visits 2nd Reserve Civil Horse lines a.m. and B.34 A25 RFA A line P.m. Received Personal Letter for inspection and one for Installations Early reply & 18th Division returns William Just afternoon of film view. Mr Baer	[signature]

WAR DIARY
~~INTELLIGENCE SUMMARY~~
(Erase heading not required.)

Army Form C. 2118.

Place	Date	Hour	Summary of Events and Information	Remarks and references to Appendices
FRESNICOURT	July 3rd -16		Routine work. Riding School. Inspection of Musketry Rd. Visits King's Horse and sent to MVS for treatment on H.D. Most possible case of Debility and Incomplete change in a true Horse. Reports it to A.D.V.S. Visits and saw several very bad Backs. Buffalo is they are. They there met. Lt. Shellimy with the Stable Management R.T.R.S. Lauleain & Allied and calls at Mess of A.O.F.S. Visits to S/R. Co 2 w/os brown and sent in to H.Q. in case of Engineers Manage. Visits by Staff Captain D.H.S. Div & Supply here.	MCGK
"	4		Routine work. A.D.V.S. inspects section and cross out the Use of transport from Steam Kung the A. H.Q. G. Mess changes. S. Visits and inspects with A.D.V.S. Lines No 5) 2nd R.G. Bn.R. Arranges for treatment and Change of men here see Lyman Skirmish Day Capt Dickinson visits Section & Surplus horses to be removed.	MCGK

WAR DIARY
INTELLIGENCE SUMMARY

Place	Date	Hour	Summary of Events and Information	Remarks and references to Appendices
FRESNICOURT	July-16 5th		Routine work. Received 15 horses and 1 mule W. Bagn-lv 73 tpt. Visits Mess of A.V.C. and Inspects will him its O/c and 2 i/c's from Visits work to Farm. Horses were sent to Berlin will sick horses and after losing sent horses. Sent by Sen who has not returned. Back by g.c.h. Horses e.g. in charges and musperin re duties of sent.R.R.	
"	6th		Routine work. Visits 3rd Reg Park and Keeps towards troops. Sent in from latter horse with shop harge. Reviews C/E halm and fresh to 7 days back up F.P. and Pte Pack to the 1.F.P. 7 days sent Latter week. in. At funtionment. Visits by Pens Woodly and 2/c Seen Duties of Sergt A.V.C. Aeknowledges receipts of works to H.Ps of R.R.	
"	7th		Routine work. Visits 3rd Reg P.C and squadron K stores. Routine work. Reports. Inspects horses 5th K.N. autogun Reg. Park. Section of Reg. P. E. inspection of 7 horses lv 4th R of Furl.	
"	8th		Area Reviews Wheelers of B horses of 3320 R Fusiliers Labor Battal Inspect. Visits hos 3. aust. fan Ambulance Receives Gen Owen's charge suffering from mange in relevant R.R.	

WAR DIARY
~~INTELLIGENCE SUMMARY~~
(Erase heading not required.)

Army Form C. 2118.

Place	Date	Hour	Summary of Events and Information	Remarks and references to Appendices
FRESNICOURT	July 9		Routine work. Visits to Div. Co. train another Co. Sect. to M.S. horses from 15.2.11 Gd. Medlin Sect.	
"	10		Routine work. Awarded 16 Chevrons 1 mile 15.113. Visits Div. & ADMS. Its Div. Co. train Section in horse lines sent in two horse injuries in	
"	11		remained in HQ Co. train. Routine work. Visits N.3 Co. train. Sent to Rechuttree unmanageable.	
"	12		Routine work. Rainy before a.m. Visits to Rec P.S. another 17 M.V. & others. Rec sore knees 15.5.11 at Chlan	
"	13		Routine work. am received 13 horses 2 males & G.A.S.S. Visits to HQ another Div. Co. train. Impressive very law. M.B. Co. joint Div. & mule Mocke OC train sent in 3 to M.S. Visits Jud Rec Par.	
"	14		Routine work. horses still wind ruffle. Inspection of Respirators. Visits ND Co another N.3 Co train with ADr. S.	

WAR DIARY
~~INTELLIGENCE SUMMARY~~
(Erase heading not required.)

Army Form C. 2118.

Place	Date	Hour	Summary of Events and Information	Remarks and references to Appendices
	July 1916			
FRESNICOURT	15th		Routine work. Mounts Parle with Rifle. Visits lines of 2 pm R. & Batt. and Diekbusch 15.2.11. Attends Conference of V.O.s at Place S	AR96R
	16th		A.M.S. and visits lines. 1 N.C.O. & tr C.O. train Detmps / Rose Visits 1st & C. train & 2nd C. h.2.C. moves to Divisné	AR96R
	17th		Routine work. Visits to Spro farm A.D.S. & an 1st Ca anst 107 Ca farm. Collects 4 horses by Ambulances. Own ration inspection. Routine work. Evacuates 33 horses and 2 mules. Allots 2 horses by Ambulance. Visits 2nd R.E. Parts ans sent M.I.H.D. & A.N.G. Visits by O.C. 4 7th and 31st Dn. h. Sept	AR96R
	18th		Routine work. Rifle Inspection. Inspection of Reformatif.	AR96R
	19th		Visits to 5rs & train. Collects There fron 4 Co. train. Changes Greeley to Duspl. Campis with 1st 2nd Co. train. Visits Ausg. at sa Gents.	AR96R
DIÉVAL	20th		Routine work. Visits all nyto 2 train. Dalmps more ?	AR96R
	21st		2 Co. Preparing to Entrain. Entrains at Clives for South. at 11 p.m. Detrains at Salient.	

Army Form C. 2118.

WAR DIARY
or
INTELLIGENCE SUMMARY.
(Erase heading not required.)

Instructions regarding War Diaries and Intelligence Summaries are contained in F. S. Regs., Part II. and the Staff Manual respectively. Title pages will be prepared in manuscript.

Place	Date	Hour	Summary of Events and Information	Remarks and references to Appendices
SALEUX	July 16 21st		Army Formation. Ambulance Moraine at Longeau. Law will to Sub Ambulance to go to Saleux. Unosil Amien 5 Davours refs encampres until all 2nd Fld Amby. Horse had chief Ephram Smiths/Brickets arrived	appx
DABOURS	22nd		Routine work. Review the Inspection of Rifle [?]. Horses. Lumpies will hot Seal A.C.	appx
"	23rd		Routine work. Evacuated 8 cases from Frankment	appx
"	24th		Routine work. Gates all on [?] train ambulance at Corbie.	
"	25th		Routine work. Sent over to Amien Abbaton [?]. Pue. Miller horse up left Ephrem in Hosp. The lat Arof Amp & no he now sine Gar. Div.	appx appx
"	26th		Routine work. Cafe & Reparator Inspection	appx
"	27th		Routine work. Service. Visits Amy Genl Niee M [?]	appx appx
BRAY	28th		Change location to Bray.	appx
"	29th		Routine work. Cleaning Saddlery and clean up fatique	appx

Army Form C. 2118.

WAR DIARY
or
INTELLIGENCE SUMMARY.
(Erase heading not required.)

Instructions regarding War Diaries and Intelligence Summaries are contained in F. S. Regs., Part II. and the Staff Manual respectively. Title pages will be prepared in manuscript.

Place	Date	Hour	Summary of Events and Information	Remarks and references to Appendices
	July-16			
BRAY	30th		Routine work. Evacuated 32 cases & 3 singles at moment & altho about 12 leaven fighting. Various all Cos. A Div. train and sent in to the 12 h VS. 3 livres	appx.
"	31st		Routine work. Rifle Inspection. Inspected all livres & Nos 2 and Lt. Cos. train of from town and Various appx. R. No. Offr and No 3 Co Ricks line. Various medals and appx. L. Dr 9th Divre	appx.

CONFIDENTIAL

WAR DIARY OF

No. 3. M.V.S.

From Aug 1st -16
to Aug 31st -16.

(Vol. 1.)

WR 23

Army Form C. 2118.

WAR DIARY
or
INTELLIGENCE SUMMARY
(Erase heading not required.)

Instructions regarding War Diaries and Intelligence Summaries are contained in F. S. Regs., Part II. and the Staff Manual respectively. Title pages will be prepared in manuscript.

Place	Date	Hour	Summary of Events and Information	Remarks and references to Appendices
Harbourin	Aug.-16 1st		Routine work. Rifle and repeater inspector. Visits all cars of train, custains & flues	
"	2nd		Routine work. Inspects lines of No 2 and 4 Co. train	
"	3rd		Routine work. Inspects lines of Gds Dit and No 3 Co. train	
"	4th		Routine work. Visits A.D.C.S. Destroys twere Supplying with Petroleum	
"	5th		Routine work. Visits Siek Line of train	
"	6th		Routine work. Inspects R.Hd. and Visits Siek Lines of trains	
"	7th		Routine work. Visits train Siek Line	
"	8th		Routine work. Inspects section lines and visits A.D.C.S.	
"	9th		Routine work. and making preparation to move.	
"	10th		Routine work. and further preparation	
DAOURS	11th		Changed location to DAOURS. Travels 92 hours horse No 72 M. V. S. hours at Daours very late	
SAILLY SUR SOMME	12th		After a very log and slow march changed location to SAILLY SUR SOMME.	

WAR DIARY or INTELLIGENCE SUMMARY

Army Form C. 2118.

Place	Date	Hour	Summary of Events and Information	Remarks and references to Appendices
St SAVEUR	Aug 13th		Changed location with train to St Sauveur.	
"	14th		Routine work. Rifle Inspection. Verbs fired.	
"	15th		Routine work. Visited VIGNACOURT and no gun location for men S.	
VIGNACOURT	16th		Changed location to VIGNACOURT	
BERNACOURT	17th		Changed location to BERNACOURT and proceeded in morris 3 lorres.	
BUS LES ARTOIS	18th		Changed location to BUS LES ARTOIS and proceeded there in Morris Lorries at CANDAS.	
"	19th		Routine work. Rifle and horse inspection.	
COUIN	20th		Changed location to COUIN and placed in most unsuitable place for men S.	
"	21st		Routine work. Visited Rifle line Stores.	
"	22nd		Routine work. Inspected horses of Nos 2, 3 & C trans	
"	23rd		Routine work. Visited DOULLENS re Models for Coys.	

WAR DIARY
or
INTELLIGENCE SUMMARY.
(Erase heading not required.)

Army Form C. 2118.

Place	Date	Hour	Summary of Events and Information	Remarks and references to Appendices
COUIN	Aug-16 M		Routine work. Reenacts 19 Lewes and 1 mule from monastent. Visits lines of 100 & fills and us grain rations loves. Infantry and Retaine Imperials Rifle inspires of No. 3 C. train	
"	25th		Routine work.	
"	26th		Routine work.	
"	27th		Routine work. Visits Field line of train ambulances	
"	28th		Routine work. Reenacts 21 horses and 1 mule from hospitals. Inspects no. 1 Sec to Horse	
"	29th		Routine work. Inspects no. 2 to horse.	
"	30th		Routine work. Inspects no. 2 to horses and visits Bilges on search for new location for No. 1 S	
"	31st		Routine work. Rifle inspection. Visits field hone line of train.	

WAR DIARY. Vol 24

OF

No 3. M.V.S.

from Sept 1st - 16 Sept 20th & 9-15 Sept.

Reconstructed

WAR DIARY
or
INTELLIGENCE SUMMARY.
(Erase heading not required.)

Army Form C. 2118.

Place	Date	Hour	Summary of Events and Information	Remarks and references to Appendices
	Sept-16			
LOUVIN	1st		Routine work. Inspected 4 Coy. of train.	AP96R
"	2nd		" Visits Park Horse Lines of nos 2,3,4 Co. train	AP96R
"	3rd		Rest. 16 Movement and renewals 27 horses	AP96R
"	4th		Routine work. Visits horse line of No 1, No 3, No 4, No 3 Co, 6 am	AP96R
"	5th		Routine work. Visits 4 Co 6.10 am	AP96R
"	6th		" Rest 15 Movement but renewals 26	AP96R
"	7th		Horse and 3 mules. Visits No 2, 4 Co 6.0 am	AP96R
"	8th		Routine work. Inspection of section horses and stables	AP96R
"	9th		" Visits No 3 and No 4 Ph Co 6.0 am	AP96R
"	10th		" Visits all Co 6.0 am	AP96R
"	11th		" Inspection of repairs and No 2 & 3 Co 6.0 am	AP96R
"	12th		" Visits No 2 & 3. Co 6 am 6.25, 6.36	AP96R
"	13th		Horse cart but renewals 16 horses	AP96R
"	14th		Routine work. Inspection of section horses	AP96R
"	15th		" Visits No Ph and No 3 Co. train	AP96R

WAR DIARY
or
INTELLIGENCE SUMMARY.
(Erase heading not required.)

Army Form C. 2118.

Place	Date	Hour	Summary of Events and Information	Remarks and references to Appendices
COUIN	Sept-16			
	15th		Routine work. Inspected Section and interviewed Fatigue for clean it. Visits all Co trains. Routine work. Changes to calm.	W881
	16th		Account of Stores. Continue work. Inspects no 2 & 4 Co trains Yates & 1/p Co train.	W881 W881
	17th		Report to Colonel and inspects A Battery Routine work. Visits no 2 & 4 Co train	W881
	18th		Continue work. Inspects 15 horses from horse field no.	W881
	19th		" Visits no 3 and 4 Co train him horse field no.	W881 W881
	20th		Continue work. Inspects horses & B Co and 1st Div train	W881 W881
	21st		" Visits Cullen Platter Rifle and Seefer horse inspection.	
	22nd		Continue work. Inspects 13 horses and 2 mules for hard cast Visits 1st Co Can Coss. Stalls reelson & mounts Stables.	W881 W881
	23rd		Continue work. Visits no 3 & 4 Co train	W881
	24th		" Inspects rifles and desperators milie @ Section	W881

Army Form C. 2118.

WAR DIARY
or
INTELLIGENCE SUMMARY.
(Erase heading not required.)

Instructions regarding War Diaries and Intelligence Summaries are contained in F. S. Regs., Part II. and the Staff Manual respectively. Title pages will be prepared in manuscript.

Place	Date	Hour	Summary of Events and Information	Remarks and references to Appendices
COUIN	Sept-16 25th		Routine work. Visits all Co. of train. Inspects	WD85
"	26th		" Inspects Nos 1 & 2 S.C. train Lieuts. Nos. 11 horses, non horse-cart.	WD86 WD87
"	27th		" Visits Nos. 3 and 4. S.C. train. Inspects	WD88
"	28th		Routine work. Instructed to visit Stationary Sections of Supply Column until further available.	
"	29th		Routine work. Inspects Nos S No. 3 S.C. train	WD89
"	30th		" Visits all S.Q. Line train. and inspects horses of No. 2. Co. Units Standing works Long Or.	WD90

WAR DIARY
or
INTELLIGENCE SUMMARY.
(Erase heading not required.)

Army Form C. 2118.

Place	Date	Hour	Summary of Events and Information	Remarks and references to Appendices
COUIN	Oct -16			
"	2nd		Routine work. Inspects 4 6=2 g Train	J.J.D.
"	3rd		" " "	J.J.D.
Vauchelles	3rd		Changes situation to Vauchelles. Evacuates 9 horses and 2 mules	J.J.D.
"	4th		Routine work. Inspects 4 6=2 g Train.	J.J.D.
"	5th		" Visits here H.B.2. Train. Evacuates 16 horses	J.J.D.
"	6th		" Inspects 3 6=2 g Train.	J.J.D.
"	7th		" Inspection of Section Horses and Mules	J.J.D.
"	8th		" Inspects 2 6=2 g Train. Evacuates 8 horses	J.J.D.
"	9th		" Visits 4 sick horses g Train	J.J.D.
"	10th		" Evacuates 9 horses	J.J.D.
"	11th		" Inspects mules and rifles	J.J.D.
"	12th		" Inspects all 6=2 g Train	J.J.D.
"	13th		" Evacuates 6 horses and 2 mules.	J.J.D.
"	14th		" Inspects 21 horses g 6th Cab. Bn.	J.J.D.
"	15th		" Inspects Section and arranges general fatigue for clean-up	J.J.D.
			No serious number of contagious disease cases during this month	J.J.D.

WAR DIARY or INTELLIGENCE SUMMARY.

Army Form C. 2118.

Mob Vely Vol 25

(Erase heading not required.)

Place	Date	Hour	Summary of Events and Information	Remarks and references to Appendices
Vauchelles	16		Routine Work. Changes locatio of Sick lines on account of mud.	99 D.
"	17		Routine Work. Inspects all 6 of Train. Evacuates 1 horse & 1 mule	99 D.
"	18		Routine Work. Evacuates 5 horses & 1 mule	99 D.
"	19		Routine Work. Visits horses of 6th Lab. Bat.	99 D.
"	20		Routine Work. Inspects 4 Co of Train	99 D.
"	21		Routine Work. Evacuates 6 horses. Moves horse lines	99 D.
"	22		" Rifles and Section horses inspects.	99 D.
"	23		" Visits 3 sick horses D. Train	98 D.
"	24		Changes situation to Bois les Autors. Evacuates 5 horses & 3 mules	99 D.
"	25		Routine work. Fatigue work arranging quarters for men & horses	99 D.
"	26		" Evacuates 35 horses	99 D.
"	27		" Inspects all Train horses	99 D.
"	28		" Evacuates 8 horses & 1 mule.	99 D.
"	29		" Section horse saddlery inspects	99 D.
"	30		" Evacuates 146 horses of 29th Div. A.S.	99 D.
"	31		" Inspects Train horses.	99 D.

Constituted Vol 26

Mer Diary
of
E. M. V. S.

from Nov't. -16 to Nov 30t -16

WAR DIARY
or
INTELLIGENCE SUMMARY

Army Form C. 2118.

Place	Date	Hour	Summary of Events and Information	Remarks and references to Appendices
BUS LES ARTOIS	Nov 1st		Routine work. Visits to various Sections.	
"	2nd		" Evacuated 4.2 horses and 2 mules	
"	3rd		" Visits to various sick lines and inspections	
"	4th		Proceed to Hdqrs Div Co.	
"	5th		Routine work. Inspected Eastern. Evacuated 21 horses and 2 mules.	
"	6th		Routine work. Inspected hrs 2 and Lt Co Pollin	
"	7th		" Evacuated 6.3 horses	
"	8th		" Inspected M.G. and reinforcements Evacuated 10 horses and 1 mule	
"	9th		" Inspected M.G. Co Lys	
"	10th		" Work to horses.	
"	11th		" Evacuated 2.2 horses and 4 mules.	
"	12th		" Visited various sick lines	
"	13th		" Inspected 2 section horse and battery 20c	
"	14th		" Visited all Co. of Brun and W.G. Nice	

WAR DIARY
or
INTELLIGENCE SUMMARY.
(Erase heading not required.)

Army Form C. 2118.

Place	Date	Hour	Summary of Events and Information	Remarks and references to Appendices
BUS LES ARTOIS	Mar 15.16		Routine work. Reinforcements 6 2 horses 6 mules	
"	16.17		" " 12 " 3 "	
"	17.17		Fatigues and repairs	
"	18.17		Routine work. Visits all Coy of Train	
"	19.17		Reinforcements 23 horses and 1 mule	
DOULLENS			Changes location to Doullens	
			Details 1 h Co with men back to H.Q. 2 m V & Jr	
			Reinforcements	
			July Mule and Du Artillery move up	
			8 horses and 3 mules	
			Changes location to Bernaville	
BERNAVILLE	22.17		Reinforcements 3 horses from Canvas	
	23.17		Changes location to Franvu	
FRANS V. M	24.17		" to Brailly	
	25.17		Routine work. Parcels M/d Visits W.B.C. to ain	
BRAILLY	26.17		Changes location to Yvrench	
YVRENCH	27.17		Changes location to Drevinville to find the Rolevis wheel	

WAR DIARY
INTELLIGENCE SUMMARY

Army Form C. 2118.

Place	Date	Hour	Summary of Events and Information	Remarks and references to Appendices
YPRES(?)CH	27th	noon	Bn has been allotted to the sector reserved by 23rd R. the has great difficulty in selecting a suitable location.	
NEUVILLE	28th		Reconnoitred and settling down in new location.	
"	29th		— Inspection of rifle and section cines. Visits	
"	30th		No 2.3.1 H.Co. Men sick Cross Lug Rouline work. Evacuates horses. Surved by road to Proven. Rly tpt. Abeeles.	

Confidential.
_____

War Diary.   Vol 27
_____

No. 3 m. V. S.
_____

From Dec 1st 1916 to Dec 31st 1916

(Vol. 1.)

WAR DIARY
INTELLIGENCE SUMMARY

Army Form C. 2118.

Place	Date	Hour	Summary of Events and Information	Remarks and references to Appendices
NEUVILLE	DEC-1st		Routine work of Section. Started hut for Company of Divisional train inspection. Inspected No 5.	
"	2nd		" Rifle inspection.	
"	3rd		Law & Cap Lowto	
"	4th		Routine work of Section. Inspected horse of No 3 Co train. Evacuated 6 horses & mules to No 5	
"	5th		22 Vety Hosp Allonne. Routine work of Section. Visited sick lines of all Cos train and inspected stable and horse of 1th Sqn G	
"	6th		Routine work. Evacuated 3 horses and 2 mules to Hospital	
"	7th		Visits by R.V.O. 8 inspected sick lines of train	
"	8th		Evacuated 12 horses. Inspected rifle and bayonet of Section	
"	9th		Routine Section work. Catching wall of object. Sent to R.V.	
"	10th		Hunter. Visited all 6th Cos horse lines of train. Routine work. Evacuated 14 horses to Vety Hospital. Inspected stable and harness of No 4 Co train	

WAR DIARY
or
INTELLIGENCE SUMMARY

Army Form C. 2118

Place	Date	Hour	Summary of Events and Information	Remarks and references to Appendices
NEUVILLE	Dec-11th		Routine work of Section. Evacuate 3 lines to Hospital. Nos. 8 proceeds to England on 10 days leave.	
"	12th		Visits all Field lines of train.	
"	13th		Routine work of Section. Capt. Dunlop acting A.D.M.S. Visits all Field lines of train and Imperlis lines of No 3 Co.	
"	14th		Routine work of Section. Rifle inspection. Visits Field lines of train.	
"	15th		Continued. Evacuates 8 cases to Hospital. Imperlis stable and lines of No 2 Company.	
"	16th		Continued. Evacuates 4 lines to Hospital. Team horse to Contrille and Berneth.	
"	17th		Routine work of Section.	
"	18th		" " Evacuates 14 lines to Hospital. Endeavour admitted to Hospital.	
"	19th		No. 9 - 6.30 am at Berneth. Routine work of Section. Rifle inspection. Visits Field lines of train.	

WAR DIARY
INTELLIGENCE SUMMARY
(Erase heading not required.)

Army Form C. 2118.

Place	Date	Hour	Summary of Events and Information	Remarks and references to Appendices
NEVILLE	Dec-16 20		Routine work of Section. Huewals 5 lures 15 to hotel	C
"	21st		" Visits all Siel, line of train	
"	22nd		" Mr C S retires from leave. Visits	
"	23rd		Nos 2. 3. 4. & 6 train	
"			Routine work of Section. Huewals 4 lures 15 to hotel	
"	24th		Visits train Siel, line.	
"	25th		Routine work. Marketing preparation for Xmas dinner	
"	26th		Xmas Day Holiday	
"			Routine work. Visits all Co. of train and 5.A.R.2.	
"	27th		" Section. Rifle and Respirator inspection	
"	28th		" Visits Nos 2. 3. 4. & 6 train	
"	29th		" Huewals 3 lures 15 to hotel	
"	30th		" Visits all Siel, line of Mountains	
"	31st		Slides of types and 5 Co. Routine work of Section. Huewals 10 lures 15 to hotel	

2ND DIVISION
DIVL. TROOPS

NO. 3 MOBILE VETY SECTION

~~JAN-DEC 1917~~

1917 JAN — 1918 DEC

Confidential
War Diary.
of
G.S.
M.E.F.

Vol 28

From Jany 1st – 17

(Vol. I)

To Jany 31st –
(Vol. I)

WAR DIARY or INTELLIGENCE SUMMARY

Army Form C. 2118.

Instructions regarding War Diaries and Intelligence Summaries are contained in F.S. Regs., Part II. and the Staff Manual respectively. Title pages will be prepared in manuscript.

(Erase heading not required.)

Place	Date	Hour	Summary of Events and Information	Remarks and references to Appendices
NEUVILLE	Jan 1st		Routine work. Evacuated 19 Horses and 2 mules	
"	2nd		" " 8 Horses. Rodes all Cos	
"	3rd		Horses at Cubville and Bernaville	
"	4th		Routine work. Inspected the Section	
"	5th		" Visits all Cos. of Train	
"	6th		" Evacuated 14 Horses	
"	7th		"	
"	8th		" 9 " and 7 mules	
"	9th		Visits all Cos of Train and Inspected Horse Shoe & Co. Evacuated 2 Horses by Motor Float to No 22 Hosp. and changed location from NEUVILLE to BERNAVILLE	
BERNAVILLE	10th		Routine work for the day. Routine work Camp on	
"	11th		Changed location to MARIEUX and Camped in a very bad place by Park.	
MARIEUX	12th		Remained Horse for one day. Routine work Camp on	

Army Form C. 2118.

WAR DIARY

Army Form C. 2118.

Place	Date	Hour	Summary of Events and Information	Remarks and references to Appendices
MARIEUX	Jan-17 13th		Changes Creation to BOUZINCOURT.	
BOUZINCOURT	14th		Marching to Bieets and Horse lines left in Jolly Stables for Journes Unit. Visits all 6.27 p.m.	
"	15th		Billo claimed up. Wagonalis 46 horses and 1 mule	
"	16th		Routine work. Inspection Repeater and Rifle Itd all Mounted Trumpets, Wagonalis 16 horse and 2 mule	
"	17th		Routine work. Inclemining tables and schemes. Rifles Drawing lands for Corporals. Additional stabling for 30 Horses. Visits Self here lines 5/7 rain Wagonalis 23 horses and 1 mule.	
"	18th		" 47 "	
"	19th		" " stables freed ready for stalling	
"	20th		" Wagonalis 37 horses. Inspection No 2 Co.Mn/Hrs	
"	21st		"	
"	22nd		" stables construction of stables and improving	
"	23rd		Nu obs claiming Routine work. Inspection Hospitals It O/c Co Train lines. Burial died lines of Worker 3 Co.	

Army Form C. 2118.

WAR DIARY
or
INTELLIGENCE SUMMARY.
(Erase heading not required.)

Instructions regarding War Diaries and Intelligence Summaries are contained in F. S. Regs., Part II. and the Staff Manual respectively. Title pages will be prepared in manuscript.

Place	Date	Hour	Summary of Events and Information	Remarks and references to Appendices
BOUZINCOURT	Jany - 17			
"	25th		Routine work. Forwards 24 cores. Sopwells the Scelion + anothers of M.B. Captain	
"	26th		Routine work. Visits all sick here lin s/morn. Forwards 26 cores.	
"	27th		-	
"	28th		Routine work. Reviews notice to move, in hopes mind will fully recover, account of congestion of base, things 3 lores. Have about 70 mins	
"	29th		Routine work. now on hand. O. B. + C. units unable to send in no more mind lin u/S unable evacuation statements anything but meating antihogin and shmore Unbury get units and there the Section	
"	30th		Routine work.	
"	31st		- Receives several more mong cases	

Vol 29

War Diary
of
No 3. M.V.S.
from Feb. 1st 1917
to Feby 28th 1917.

Confidential

(Vol 1.)

Army Form C. 2118.

WAR DIARY
or
INTELLIGENCE SUMMARY.
(Erase heading not required.)

Place	Date	Hour	Summary of Events and Information	Remarks and references to Appendices
BOUZINCOURT	Feb -7 1st	—	Routine work and work on new stables & tramroads. Owing to congestion of line of communication about 30 horses in N.T.D. train.	C
"	" 2nd	—	Routine work & Rifle and Bayonet competition. Visits all ref. Exercising & training.	B – Rifle comp
"	" 3rd	—	Routine work. Visited all Coy lines during Morning.	C
"	" 4th	—	" "	C
"	" 5th	—	Inspection not to train horses. Visit all Coy lines and inspected	C
"	" 6th	—	Lines & Stables. Inspection Parade. Routineworks. Visits all Coy lines of Morning, not inspected all lines Horses & harness	C
"	" 7th	—	Routinework. Starting on training. Visited all yards ref, Church Morning.	C
"	" 8th	—	Inspected horses & harness out of 5 lines of Morain. Proceeded to Sub-laws to 10 days leave.	

Army Form C. 2118.

WAR DIARY
or
~~INTELLIGENCE SUMMARY~~

(Erase heading not required.)

Instructions regarding War Diaries and Intelligence Summaries are contained in F. S. Regs., Part II. and the Staff Manual respectively. Title pages will be prepared in manuscript.

Place	Date	Hour	Summary of Events and Information	Remarks and references to Appendices
BOUZINCOURT	Feb 9th-17		Lieut Blake completes instruction before handing over to them. Capt Dunlop M.C. in temporary charge of Section.	C
	10th		Routine work.	
	11th	"	"	
	12th	"	16 rounds shrapnel / Bags 1 totsl	
	13th	"	"	
	14th	"	"	
	15th	"	40 rounds shrapnel	
	16th	"	"	
	17th	"	27 rounds shrapnel	
	18th	"	"	
	19th	"	"	
	20th	"	32 rounds shrapnel	
	21st	"	"	
	22nd	"	22 rounds shrapnel	B.B. Callender Capt.

WAR DIARY
INTELLIGENCE SUMMARY

Army Form C. 2118.

Place	Date	Hour	Summary of Events and Information	Remarks and references to Appendices
BOOZINCOURT	Feb 23. 17		Routine work. 21 animals /recruits/ that to hospital	
"	24.		" " "	
"	25.		" " "	
"	26.		27 animals /recruits/	
"	27.		" " "	
"	28.		32 animals /recruits/ Returns	
"			now have our look new charge of section	

Confidential

Vol 30

Mesopotamia
of
M V G
to
from March 1st 1917. to March 31st 1917.

(Vol. 1)

Army Form C. 2118.

WAR DIARY
or
~~INTELLIGENCE SUMMARY.~~
(Erase heading not required.)

Instructions regarding War Diaries and Intelligence Summaries are contained in F. S. Regs., Part II. and the Staff Manual respectively. Title pages will be prepared in manuscript.

Place	Date	Hour	Summary of Events and Information	Remarks and references to Appendices
BOUZINCOURT	March 1st-17		Routine work. Inspected all sick lines of Coln	
	2nd			
	3rd		Inspected 60 Horses and 7 mule	
	4th		Inspected sick lines & train	
			Rifle and Respirator Inspection	
	5th		Arrival of New OC and went to train	
			Routine work	

WAR DIARY
or
INTELLIGENCE SUMMARY

Army Form C. 2118.

Place	Date	Hour	Summary of Events and Information	Remarks and references to Appendices
March 1917				
OUZINCOURT	6		Routine work. Hauling manure. Removal of Scales. Routine orders on account of lessening strength in the work. Evacuated 33 animals. Visits O/C 6.S. Div. & Albert. Impeelis all lines of 112 Co. Auto-sel & line.	
	7		All C. rain.	
			Routine work. Special attention paid to repair of harness and sword. Accumulates manure. Visits 60 siel line. Inspeelis Rifles. Routine work. Visits all siel & annual & train.	
	8		" "	
	9		" "	
	10		Evacuates 61 annuals to Albert- Stn. Visits A.D.S. Impeelis 112 Div. la troas. Routine work. Visits siel line & train.	
	11		"	
	12		Hauling manure. Visits all siel	
	13		Loose line & train. Evacuate 6 train Cages to H.V. Routine work. Amounts 55 animals & base to	

WAR DIARY
or
INTELLIGENCE SUMMARY.

Army Form C. 2118.

Place	Date	Hour	Summary of Events and Information	Remarks and references to Appendices
	March			
BOUZINCOURT	14th		Routine work. Visits sick cases of Pulham	
	15th		" "	
	16th		" "	
	17th		Evacuals 4 Horses and 4 mules	
	18th		Rifle and Gas Drill. Inspection of section	
	19th		Routine work. Company Horse Shewing	
	20th		" visits sick line of Lieut [?]	
	21st		Evacuals 3 Horses and 1 mule	
	22nd		Inspects all Horses of No 3 & No. [?]	
	23rd		" " " No. 2 & No. [?]	
	24th		Inspects horses of section and	
CONTAY	25th		Routine work. Preparations for move.	
BEAUVAL	26th		Changes location to Contay	
			Routine work and changes location to Beauval	

WAR DIARY
or
INTELLIGENCE SUMMARY.
(Erase heading not required.)

Army Form C. 2118.

Place	Date	Hour	Summary of Events and Information	Remarks and references to Appendices
	March			
BOUQUE MAISON	27th		Routine work and changed location to BOUQUE MAISON	
			Rifle Inspection. Inspected lines. Went to aeri.	
RAMECOURT	28th		Routine work. Changed location to RAME COURT.	
"	29th			
PERNES	30th		Changed location to PERNES	
"	31st		Routine work. Rifle Inspection. Visited by A.P.	
			Ambulance and no 2 Co. train pick horse lines	

W.P.C. Robinson
Capt. & i/c
Army Vet. Corps

Confidential
War Diary
of
No 3 Mobile Veterinary Section.

From April 1st 1917
To April 30th 1917

Vol 31

(Vol. 1)

WAR DIARY
INTELLIGENCE SUMMARY
(Erase heading not required.)

Army Form C. 2118.

Instructions regarding War Diaries and Intelligence Summaries are contained in F. S. Regs, Part II. and the Staff Manual respectively. Title pages will be prepared in manuscript.

Place	Date	Hour	Summary of Events and Information	Remarks and references to Appendices
	APRIL 1917			
PERNES	1st		Routine work of Section. Evacuates 15 lorries and 3 mules to No 22 Base Hospital.	
"	2nd		Routine work of Section. Inspected horses of No 2 and 3 Cos. Evacuates 4 H.B. Section. Evacuates 3 mules to No 22 H.B. Routine work of Section. Inspected saddlery and harness.	
"	3rd		"	
"	4th		"	
"	5th		Inspected horses of S.A.A. Sect. D.A.C.	
"	6th		"	
"	7th		Evacuates 17 horses and 3 mule to No 22	
"	8th		Making preparations for move of 3rd Section. Change location to Monchy Breton.	
MONCHY BRETON	8th		Visits Cross of 6th & Field Ambulances	
"	9th		Cleaning up billets. Evacuates 24 horses from 2nd DAC to No 22. Inspected sick lines of 6th & 7th Ambulance and No 3 Co. 2nd D.A.C.	
HAUTE AVESNES	10th		Change location to Haute Avesnes. Visits Sick lines of each sect.	
	11th		Cleaning up billets. Routine work of Section.	

WAR DIARY
or
INTELLIGENCE SUMMARY
(Erase heading not required.)

Army Form C. 2118.

Place	Date	Hour	Summary of Events and Information	Remarks and references to Appendices
HAUTE AVESNES	APRIL 1917 12th		Routine work of Section - Visits picketlines of Nos 2, 3 and 4 Cos and train	
"	13th		Railwork. Section Inspects rifles. Visits Nos 2, 3, and 4 Co.	
"	14th		Visits No. 2, 3, 4 Cos train and inspects all	
"			Arrival of Nos 3 Co. Preparing to move on 15th	
BRAY	15th		Section changes location to Bray and places in most unsuitable billets for own section	
"	16th		Cleaning up gully riffles	
"	17th		- Routinework. Intervals HQ	
"	18th		Moves out 1 mile to 1st Canadian W.S. adding to Railway Section near Mount Capelle	
"	19th		Routine work. Swallows 31 loose and 1 mule to C.M.V.S Inspects rifles and field lines of No. 2, 3, 4 Coms.	
"	20th		" Swallows by losses and 1 mule to C. Can S.	
"	21st		Routine work Swallows 27 - 3 - 1 - -	
"	22nd		Section leaves bivouacs and wells up gullies of 4th Cops	

Army Form C. 2118.

WAR DIARY
or
INTELLIGENCE SUMMARY
(Erase heading not required.)

Instructions regarding War Diaries and Intelligence Summaries are contained in F. S. Regs., Part II. and the Staff Manual respectively. Title pages will be prepared in manuscript.

Place	Date	Hour	Summary of Events and Information	Remarks and references to Appendices
	APRIL 1917			
BRAY	22.		Railless evacuation. W.B.	
ECOIVRES	23.		Routine work. Cleaning up and building line. Scouts out suitable location- evacuate 113 lines and 13 mules	
			to 96 Velg. Hospital	
	24.		Routine work. Building horse lines. Improving stables etc.	
	25.		" "	
	26.		Visits horse lines of 115 Dn. C. 9nd Train and 6th J Ambulance	
	27.		Routine work. evacuate 35 horses and 3 mules.	
	28.		" Rifle and gallery inspection	
	29.		" evacuate 115 horses and 4 mules to No.22 Vet.	
	30.		" Visits field line and inspects all horse of H.Q. 6th Div.	
			evacuate 9.8 horses and 2 mules.	

Confidential.

W.G.S. Diary Vol 32
of
Henry S
From May 1st 1911 to May 31st 1911.

(Vol I)

WAR DIARY
or
INTELLIGENCE SUMMARY.
(Erase heading not required.)

Army Form C. 2118.

Place	Date	Hour	Summary of Events and Information	Remarks and references to Appendices
ECOIVRES	MAY-17 1st		Routine work. Visits Rbry and Infantry. Visits XIII Corps M.G. and Anti-Aircraft Schools.	
"	2d		Routineworks. Wavrans 12 lorries. 8 mules	
"	3d		" " " " 15 " 3 "	
"	4th		Inspects M/G and Trenchmortars. Wavrans 65 lorries 5 mule	
"	5th		Visits XIII Corps R.E. at Hermaville Wavrans 392 lorries 8 mule	
"	6th		Inspects section showing for saddles Wavrans 40 horses and 1 mule	
"	7th		Visits Corps Cavalry and Cyclist Bn.	
"	8th		Wavrans 35 horses and 1 mule	
"	9th		Inspects all section billets. Seems	
"	10th			
"	11th			
"	12th			

Army Form C. 2118.

WAR DIARY
or
INTELLIGENCE SUMMARY.
(Erase heading not required.)

Instructions regarding War Diaries and Intelligence Summaries are contained in F. S. Regs., Part II. and the Staff Manual respectively. Title pages will be prepared in manuscript.

Place	Date	Hour	Summary of Events and Information	Remarks and references to Appendices
ECOIVRES	May			
	13		Routine work. Visits hot rectn to Re Pol<lore lines. Starts 400 12m Lathings Cylinders for the Canopy North Trench - here - in Lord Kitsage. Having Sawpits-from Canadian Forestry Camp for logging the	W.H.Collins Capt RE
	14		Routine work. Available 76 horses and 2 mules.	
	15.5.17		" Inspects lydiat lines. Available 129 horses and 12 mules.	
	16.5.17		" Available 129 horses and 12 mules.	
	17.5.17		" Visits Corps Cavalry lines.	
	18.5.17		" RE attenuend	
	19.5.17		" Available 43 Cons. and 74 mules.	
	20		" Inspects Ly Garrison Div S. and Capt Martin D.A.D.S. 1st Army	

WAR DIARY
or
INTELLIGENCE SUMMARY

Army Form C. 2118.

(Erase heading not required.)

Instructions regarding War Diaries and Intelligence Summaries are contained in F. S. Regs., Part II. and the Staff Manual respectively. Title Pages will be prepared in manuscript.

Place	Date	Hour	Summary of Events and Information	Remarks and references to Appendices
ECOIVRES	21/1		Routine work. Marerals 35 lives and 2 mules	
	22nd		" " Inspected declarations and rifles	
	23rd		" " Marerals 36 lives and 9 mules	
	24th		" " Visits H.Q. Corps	
	25th		" " Corps Cavalry and Gelatio	
	26th		" " Marerals 46 horses 3 mules	
	27th		" " Inspected cyclist lines and T.O.	
	28th		Transport Rifles Cavalry. Visits H.Q. Corps Coys	
	29th		Routine work. "	
	30th		" " Marerals 20 horses and 2 mules	
	31st		Routine work. Visits Corps Cavalry and 5th July Unhamer horselines	

2449 Wt. W14957/M90 750,000 1/16 J.B.C. & A. Forms/C.2118/12.

Mr. Drew
of
N. Y.

No 3.

From June 1st–17
to June 30th–17

Vol 33

(No 1)

WAR DIARY
or
INTELLIGENCE SUMMARY

Army Form C. 2118.

No 3 Mobile Veterinary Section

Place	Date	Hour	Summary of Events and Information	Remarks and references to Appendices
ECOIVRES	June 1917 1st		Routine work. Train of Cols 15 Offrs 14 — Evacuated 17 animals to Base	C
	2nd		"	
	3rd		Evacuated 17 animals to Base	21
	4th		"	14
			"	52
			"	10
			"	49

Army Form C. 2118.

WAR DIARY
or
~~INTELLIGENCE~~ SUMMARY.
(Erase heading not required.)

Instructions regarding War Diaries and Intelligence Summaries are contained in F. S. Regs., Part II. and the Staff Manual respectively. Title pages will be prepared in manuscript.

Place	Date	Hour	Summary of Events and Information	Remarks and references to Appendices
Ecoivres	Jan 10/17		Routine Work	C. & etc.
"	11th		"	
"	12th		"	
"	13th		"	
"	14th		Invoerate 35 Onime 5 Bett	
"	15th		Relief. Moved to Bethune	
"	16th		Routine Work	
Bethune	17th		"	
"	18th		"	
"	19th		"	21
"	20th		"	
"	21st		"	
"	22nd		"	
"	23rd		Invested 4 Onine & Bagn	
"	24th		"	
"	25th		"	

H.Q.
 2nd Div.

Herewith War Diary of
No 3 M.V.S. for month
of July 1917

A.R.B. Richmond
Capt. V.C.
O.C. No 3. M.V.S.

Vol. 34

Mrs Grant
of M. V. B.

From July 1st 1917 to July 31st 1917

(Vol 5)

Army Form C. 2118.

WAR DIARY
or
INTELLIGENCE SUMMARY
(Erase heading not required.)

Instructions regarding War Diaries and Intelligence Summaries are contained in F. S. Regs., Part II. and the Staff Manual respectively. Title pages will be prepared in manuscript.

Place	Date	Hour	Summary of Events and Information	Remarks and references to Appendices
	July 1917			
BETHUNE	1st		Routine work. Casualties 20 wounded by barrage	
"	2nd		" Dipped 415 Tunnel	
"	3rd		" Casualties 3 wounded. Dipped 298	
"	4th		" Rifles and steel helmet inspection. Baths	
"	5th		Large line of 145 Gs Coy train. Casualties 24 wounded by barrage	
"	6th		Routine work " Dipped 412 Coming	
"	7th		" " Casualties 10 wounded by barrage. Baths	
"	8th		Out Inspection all lines of 145 Bs and? the Sur rain Routine work. Shrapnel barrage by 145 Gr Co men	
"	9th		" Casualties 3 Cases evacuated or nerves	

T2131. Wt. W708-776. 500000. 4/15. Sir J. C. & S.

WAR DIARY
or
INTELLIGENCE SUMMARY.

Army Form C. 2118.

Place	Date	Hour	Summary of Events and Information	Remarks and references to Appendices
Bethune	July 1917 9th		Took over Command of Sectn. Capt McLennand proceeded on leave.	
	10th		Routine work of Sectn. ADMS & DADVS inspected Sectn. Inspected transport cart.	
	11th		Routine work of Sectn. inspected billets rest horse. Visited horse lines of 41st Bde RFA	
	12th		Routine work of Sectn. Evacuated 12 horses & 5 mules. Rifle inspection. Examined scrapings from hospit cases, also fresh scrapings & stools. Visited DAC. H.2 with DADVS. also 14th & 74th & 75th Bdes horse lines.	
	13th		Routine work of Sectn. Prepared bed for use on 14th July/w with road officer.	
	14th		Routine work of Sectn. Evacuated 16 horses 17 mules. 13 Annual but stamps dip. Visited horse lines of 41st Bde superd RFA	
	15th		Routine work of Sectn. 8 horses from SAA. Relr disposed DDVS visited Sectn.	
	16th		Routine work of Sectn. Saddle inspection. Visited 9th Bde wagon lines.	
	17th		Routine work of Sectn. 4 horses through dip. Subovened DADVS Sectn. Future envoyay second from road trips	

WAR DIARY
or
INTELLIGENCE SUMMARY
(Erase heading not required.)

Army Form C. 2118.

Place	Date	Hour	Summary of Events and Information	Remarks and references to Appendices
Bellune	July 19.17			
	18th		Routine work of Relief. Evacuated 11 horses. 3/2 Annual Thumb dip. Repairs to road.	
	19th		Moving to dip Commenced.	
			Routine work of Relief. Sgt. Helmet euspholin. Rolid. 600m. lines 9/41st Bde R.Fg	Off. N/S
	20th		Routine work of Relief. 10 ammunce Thumb dips. Rolid. 100 4th Field Ambulance	
			Transport kind.	
	21st		Routine work of Relief. 75 tigers Thumb dips. Rolied. 41st Bde RFA hopper lines	
	22nd		Routine work of Relief. 23 horses V. 9 mules evacuated. 6 tiger Thumb dip.	
	23rd		Routine work of Relief. Rifle euspholin. also cook house Relief, 9 horses	
			Thumb dip. Rolid. 100 f.m. lines K/41st Bde RFA.	[signature]

Army Form C. 2118.

WAR DIARY
or
INTELLIGENCE SUMMARY.
(Erase heading not required.)

Instructions regarding War Diaries and Intelligence Summaries are contained in F. S. Regs., Part II. and the Staff Manual respectively. Title pages will be prepared in manuscript.

Place	Date	Hour	Summary of Events and Information	Remarks and references to Appendices
	July 1917			
BETHUNE	24th		Routine work. Evacuations and Cases of Section. Visits Cove line 5/16 Fuld Amb. Inspects Billets.	
"	25th		Routine work. Visits Cove line 57 No 2 aus 3 Cas Poslin	
"	26th		" Evacuations 8 during 24 hrs. Visits to 9/16 Fd Amb Cove line and Set in two loris at F.S.	
"	27th		Routine work. Rifle Inspection. Visits Cove line 6th Fuld Ambulance No 2 aus 3 Cas Train and large S. Nicce	
"	28th		Routine work. Evacuations 10 during... Deposits 161 hors	
"	29th		Routine work. Visits Cove line 2/16 Div Cas Train and 242 m.g.c.	
"	30th		Routine work. Visits Cove line 9 No 2 aus 3 Cas Train Evacuations 7	
"	31st		Routine work. Visits Cove line of 6th Fuld Ambulance 242 m.g.c. and 1/6 Dh Cas Train Evacuations two hors with Sick	

Mrs. Brown Vol 35
of
Mrs. M. V. Breton

from June 1st 1917 to July 31st 1917

Army Form C. 2118.

WAR DIARY
or
INTELLIGENCE SUMMARY.
(Erase heading not required.)

Instructions regarding War Diaries and Intelligence Summaries are contained in F. S. Regs., Part II. and the Staff Manual respectively. Title pages will be prepared in manuscript.

Place	Date	Hour	Summary of Events and Information	Remarks and references to Appendices
BETHUNE	Aug. 1917 1st		Routine work of Section. Evacuate 7 cases hung by Rail Ehrs 32 Hospital Look over Duties of ADMS who forwards Leaves. Visits Lieu eins of No Qtr Co. train and Bn 2 h Q C	C.
"	2nd		R. Work. Superintend loading of Motor Barge. Evacuate 6 wounded from this Section by gt-class (H.S.23 Hosp) D.D.M.S 1st Army calls at Section to discuss the question of Cage Stopping Vale which 9 have recommended in Boulogne.	B.2.3.
"	3rd		to the Running Vale with the A.D.C. for the treatment of harsh filled cases have s/t and Sludge by Moral. Visits Vlies of A.D.M.S and No It and 1 See them running 15 May 5 on arrival not each Co	3.3.
"	4th		R. Work filled in Cere of H.3rd Bty Ly ford- and 1 where from CDCS 1st Army for filler. Visits Cere eins of 6.7 Ambulance and Divest Sanits.	C.
"	5th		R. Work. Visits Vlies of Dir go S. and attends Conference of Q.V.S. at Vlies of ADS. XI Corps. Visits Cere eins of No 2 and 3 Co Tram.	33. 55.
"	6th		After 10 animes 9/46th Divison at h.g 8	
"	7th		R Work. Evacuate 28 animes by Barge (H.6.23) Hosp. Visits Vlies of DarmsS ADMS. 6.7 Amb and Inspt Co Tram.	3.5.

T2134. Wt. W708—776. 500000. 4/15. Sir J.C. & S.

Army Form C. 2118.

WAR DIARY
or
INTELLIGENCE SUMMARY.
(Erase heading not required.)

Instructions regarding War Diaries and Intelligence Summaries are contained in F. S. Regs., Part II. and the Staff Manual respectively. Title pages will be prepared in manuscript.

Place	Date	Hour	Summary of Events and Information	Remarks and references to Appendices
	Aug. 1917			
BETHUNE	6th		R. work. Visits Offrs of A & B Coys. Inspects animals of No 1 Co train and 249 h.q.C. Sent in one horse from train. Mrs S.	
"	7th		R. work. Visits Offrs of No 4 Co. S. and Aus S. I. Corps. Inspects horses of 6 C.F. Ambulance. Assists at parading of horses. Chief Vet Surgeon of 1st Army. Mrs S.	
"	"		Surgeon at work. Mrs S.	
"	8th		R. work. Visits Offrs S. Hos Chee van Offrs S 1st Army at also Offrs of horse-dracenals by Sergt. 10 animals. Visits Offrs of Aus S. and CF gas Div. in Sgtn. Chargs to Walsiel. R. Slim Dresses. Visits horselines No 1 Co train and No 2 Duwar. No 3 section N.Q.C. to inspect 2 animals. Inspects of transport. Also visits lines of No 2 and 3 Co train. Collects evidence by first for such who floains at No 1 S. also all N.Q. Cross. Saw N.q.C. gas Div Chargs	
"	9th		R. work. Visits Offrs of Aus S. Inspects Remounts at New Beef Dep. and visits horse lines of No 3 and 4 train.	
"	10th		R. work. Visits lines of 249 h.q.C. No 4 Aus Co train and Offrs of Aus S. I Corps and Bus S. train Section wastn 39 h.q.C.	

WAR DIARY or INTELLIGENCE SUMMARY

Army Form C. 2118.

Place	Date	Hour	Summary of Events and Information	Remarks and references to Appendices
BETHUNE	August 1917 10th (cont)		Repairs at huts & hut for recuperation for ranks. Remade by the Sewer. Colonels tour by float. Return from O. & Pty. R. Work. Inspects hut. St. Inflames. Materials 16 animals.	
"	11th		Afternoon wires. Colonels tour by float. November visits O/Ree C Coys. S. visits Dune cure of Hut Co tram and 7k2 N.Q.E.	
"	12th		Blunk Onspects Rifles and Saddlery of section. Visits O/Ree of and Dune cure of H.Q. Sewer and repaired R.E.	
"	13th		Blunk visits O.C. & O.S. O/Ree No. 2. 3. 4 Co Drain	
"	14th		Blunk Inspects 10 animals by Serge Colletis by float St Cure. from Hd Qr C. Drain Hants arry to Pause ? Gn off leave.	
"	15th		R. Work visits Q.r. Claudes taking cure of permanent refers. her Dy C S Civil Army O.C. S/Corps and Serge. Son S Survey. Dispatches 2.30 over for 1st Corps Cavalry. Slum badly injured while coming high days and unable to return. he N.O praced with the Nucir Ryfords hut Matt. to Dr and C.S took over x/chy Charge of 22 Co R.H. visits nos 2. 3. 4 Co Drain.	

WAR DIARY
or
INTELLIGENCE SUMMARY

Army Form C. 2118.

(Erase heading not required.)

Place	Date	Hour	Summary of Events and Information	Remarks and references to Appendices
BETHUNE	August 1917 16th		R. Work. Avacrates 12 animals by Barge. Had to suspend delousing operation on account of high percentage of injuries. Animals passing through Berlin halted near Bruay.	
"	" 17th		Lifting the matter of rate on Convalescents V.6½/c 1st Corps Cavalry called re two injured animals which were removed by him for first aid. R. Work. Evacuates 6 B.T. Ambulance. Visited to X Corps Avacuates to H.Q.S. Australians. A no of heavy shell came in between	
"	" 18th		R. Work. Surplus horses of Division sent to AV.S. for redistribution. Visits Evacuates to No 2 - 3. Co. from	
"	" 19th		R. Work. Evacuates 17 animals by Barge. Also 6 animals for VAC. Station from Ralph. animals sent to Say foreman. met N.D.V.S. at No 1. Co from and Mespels horses	
"	" 20th		R. Work. Mespels animals of Nos 5 ans 5226 5 Co R.F.A. Sent in V.S. or animals from 226 Co.	
"	" 21st		R. Work. Handling Rubble Mespels horses of No 2 3 Co	
"	" 20		R. Work. Handling Rubble for whom of standing the avacuates 16 animals	

Army Form C. 2118.

WAR DIARY
or
INTELLIGENCE SUMMARY.
(Erase heading not required.)

Instructions regarding War Diaries and Intelligence Summaries are contained in F. S. Regs., Part II. and the Staff Manual respectively. Title pages will be prepared in manuscript.

Place	Date	Hour	Summary of Events and Information	Remarks and references to Appendices
BETHUNE	August 1917			
	22nd (cont)		Embarge. Visits lines of 6th & Amb.	
	23rd		R work. Visits lines of all Cos, train and MT of C	
	24th		R work. Hawking Rifle and Whit-training. Payer at section Imperch	
	25th		Lines of 6th & Ambulance	
	26th		R work, Whit-training Stable. Visits Mess of Reay S	her Cols
			evidence and had a free chat who claims FMNS to view Yak	
			Visits 1st Capt Souilly Mess Snipping Chanda. Visits by CRS 2	
	27th		1st Corps on Yak. Materials fanned Enj Bazger.	
	28th		R work. Rifle and bne by Maj. Road from Reay Mjr 1st Cu. Ais. Impech	
			Section Rifles and Refractive. Visits by OIS P. 1st army for selection	
			Camp for Mess of his ht. for nurses	
	29th		R work. Impech lines of No 9 to 63 & N train and 9 & 2 to RC	
	30th		R work. Visits by Majs S 1st Corps on Yak	
			Sent B Gerblin lines to Runaria Marcelta lines of his Co	
			train and 242 R.E.C. Section with WS	
	31st		R work. Hawking Rifle and Whit-training. Visits lives in	
			6th & Amb and No I.C. W. Borm	

Army Form C. 2118.

WAR DIARY
or
INTELLIGENCE SUMMARY.
(Erase heading not required.)

Instructions regarding War Diaries and Intelligence Summaries are contained in F. S. Regs., Part II. and the Staff Manual respectively. Title pages will be prepared in manuscript.

Place	Date	Hour	Summary of Events and Information	Remarks and references to Appendices
	August 1915			
BETHUNE	30th		R. went. Visited Ourselves & Nos 2 and 3 Cas. Stat. and 242 h.F.C. Inspection of Rifles (Civil St. Luch and Reparation Arsenales 32 lines Infantry (Grs) 33 Hospital	
"	"		R. went. Called to hot Corpsman. Visited Ourselves. 1, 2 and 3 Cas. and 242 h.F.C.	
"	31st		Inspection arrived S. 1st & Amb. Lance	

Vol 36

Mrs Brown
from N.Y.S.
20 Sept 30th 1917

Noel

From Sept 1st 1917

WAR DIARY / INTELLIGENCE SUMMARY

Army Form C. 2118.

Place	Date	Hour	Summary of Events and Information	Remarks and references to Appendices
BETHUNE	September 1917			
	1st		Patients took wounded & sick to No 2 (?) Base Hospital by Barge. Patients here line of No 2 [?] train and 6.52 p.m.	
	2nd		R Wards. Visits line of No 2 & No 1. D.G. Evac [?] and No 3 C [?] train. W [?] Lunch Maj [Lowe?] F. Lances sent everyone No 2 B Train by [?] per impedia	
			The Referees wounded & Wells by that was in Matty Gaston [?] follows	
	3rd		R Wards. Visits by Nurses SB. Wells time by that from train. Half one [?] there to her Civil Section. Mattinson arrived. [?] No 2 C Pictile [?] Welle [?]	
	4th		use of No 2 C train. Inspection Section R.E.R. [?] R Wards. Both Matton upon Serchine of No 2 C train Sections [?] Lieu Inspection of [?] train Visits lines of No 3 C.C. from Welles [?] Lunch for 10th Hugal Filler. Visits by B/N.S. 101 and AD.D.S. Three	
	5th		Inspectors of wounded of No 12 and C Mallison (various [?] R.Wards. Inspected 24 wounded by Barge. E.E. Callen 246 Callen [?]	
	6th		& Billet at No 2 C train. Visits line of 6th [?] No 2 & No 3 [?] [?] [?] R Wards. Visits line of No 1, 2, & 3 C train arriving for C. Evacue [?] Receipts from M.E.O. of M.E. Kitchener Works [?] for Berry/[?] Visits by Maj G.S.O. & Buisville. [?] [?]	

WAR DIARY
or
INTELLIGENCE SUMMARY.
(Erase heading not required.)

Army Form C. 2118.

Place	Date	Hour	Summary of Events and Information	Remarks and references to Appendices
	September 1917.			
BETHUNE 7th			R.work. Visits by A.D.V.S. & Capt. Walsh also by O.C. 1st Army and I.D. horses to Ruminghem and returns. 3 returns submits statistical report & Adjoint operations carried out by the section for period June 29th to July 6th week. Strength of unit = 33. 1.6 horses & Mules.	E.B.
	8th		Amb. and Vet. bus of No 2 & 3 Co train	E.B.
	9th		R.work. Visits by A.D.V.S. & Capt. Walsh. Vets bus of 6 & 7 A.N.	(illegible)
	10th		R.work. Visits from Vets. of No 2 & 3 Co train	E.B.
			R.work. Attends glees of Maj. & O.C. Vety. Hosp. at A.D. & St Pol. Calls at Vet. sectn. Vets bus of No 1.6 horses and 1/2 h of C. Zou.	E.B.
	11th		In hands of A.D.V.S. for refresher course of Calaumes.	
			R.work. Evacuates 7 horses by Barge. Visits bourlues of No 3 Co bn. and Calls at No 1 Resident Section in charge.	E.B.
	12th		R.work. Hauling Rubble. Sends A.R. of 2 horses to the (illegible) at Loos. Returns charge of O.C. 2nd Dn. Downeys ND of no 3 6 hairs inward bar lice of Section since June 9th inst. Infirmy per Inspector Palestine.	E.B.
			Pel. Muslim. Oxellous Calender weighing B/u/b

WAR DIARY
or
INTELLIGENCE SUMMARY

(Erase heading not required.)

Army Form C. 2118.

Place	Date	Hour	Summary of Events and Information	Remarks and references to Appendices
BÉTHUNE	September 1917 12th	(cal)	Visits base lines of 242 & Cas. 1st Co. train Called there by Flash Spr. Amery. Walk to New York station by 1st Corps R.E.	See Sept 23
"	13th		Rwork. Visits Nos 2 & 3 Co. train. 6th Am. Ammn 242. L.C. Left to hunt for Letty unit at Walmer at St Cecil Sr.	
"	14th		Rwork. Walnut & Tunnel by Bosch. Called here from post Foot. Gas section Visits Mess of Mays S. Impeels lines of 6th Aml.	
"	15th		Rwork. Railway Rubble. Visits by Mays S. Impeels lines of 1146. 9th Co. train and 242. W.G.C.	
"	16th		Rwork. Railway Rubble. Impeels lines of 6th Z. Aml.	
"	17th		Rwork. Visits by Rt. Amfg. 2nd Div. num. falls about Meuse & Visits lines 9 hrs 9 Co. train and Impeels lines 9 No.3 Co. train	
"	18th		Rwork. Railway Rubble. Visits by Mays S. into Railg. 2nd Div. 7th new falling. Impeels lines of 15th Ams. Visits lines of 242 h.p. and 116 h.p. Co. train	
"	19th		Rwork. Visits by Mr. S. XI Corps. Reports that Horty of 251 Rz. Surveying Co. Sgt. in Welch Guns Shore sent troop hauge hit.	

Army Form C. 2118

WAR DIARY
or
INTELLIGENCE SUMMARY.
(Erase heading not required.)

Place	Date	Hour	Summary of Events and Information	Remarks and references to Appendices
	September 1917			
BETHUNE	10th	(cont)	Wheels by float. Ant. Echoys Lucie & 2 D.A.C. by lorry from Treuil. Sent 3 cylinders lorries to Rennescure & and Walch No 2 - 3 Co Ammn. Column. Columns here by float from over. Vicks by O.C. N°37 M.V.C. & swamming party, arrived by 0.0083, also by A.D.C. 1st Corps. r V.C. projects were ST. ot ANG. Mallein tests trued. 9/10 from 14 sections Live Hd. Quen [illegible] in Durval lines. No Reach. Fix mare after injection by Liaut Down Road Peripheral intra temp 103°F Intrathoracic mallein and some local swelling. mal Declarge off side Ruck inoculated 10 unmed. by large. After 2 hours temp 105°F and by [illegible] Mallein to Mallein test. sent to Reserve seclum. [illegible] [illegible] injns by lin. hr of Adj. hot. Lan Garoche Reports to Dad. S.G. Lippers injns by lin. Reput from Rennesure, Aus Estren. Noes one of W3.C. came Runsch. of wheels loss by float from hat. Vickd. from Reserve. Rad. inopculus. 202 L.B.C hrs 1-2 ½ by tram. Visits by A.D.C. & Lt Cope and [illegible] [illegible] treval. V.C.Y. Wright Cantr. called in treval. Roxy

WAR DIARY or INTELLIGENCE SUMMARY

Army Form C. 2118

Place	Date	Hour	Summary of Events and Information	Remarks and references to Appendices
BETHUNE	September 1917			
	23rd		Routine work. Vailis Rowline of 1/6th F. Amb and 2/3 C. Train. Wounded 12 horses by bomb.	
	24th		Routine. Stationary Rifle. Vehicles broken. Vehicles broken by lorry. Vailis by bombing party on train. Evacuated routine 1st 60/10 m/Val. & Vailis line of Anglier by Bu (9c)	
	25th		Fuels ambulance	
	26th		Routine work. Evacuated 5 animals by lorry. Vailis lines of No.1, 2, 3 C. train ans 242 in O.C. Sent in the horse for 1/9 O men.	
	27th		N.S. Vailes by No. ADS&B ans 242 & Resp. of W.Yet.	
			Vailes horselines & No. 1, 2, 3 Co. trains ans 242. N.Q. for line from M.D. Co. train for evacuation.	
	28th		Routine. Vailes lines of No6 Fuels ambulance, No. Sewell to change Pickets. Truck Vehmen and Williams.	
	29th		Routine Vailes Co. 1, 2, 3 Co. Train. Truck Vehmen and William. Called to Truck for maclov 5 Mallen	
	30th		Routine work. Truck fry remove for Evacuator. Evacuated 5 animals by train. Inspected lines of 1/6 & 7 Ambulance. Received 3 animals	

Army Form C. 2118.

WAR DIARY
or
INTELLIGENCE SUMMARY.
(Erase heading not required.)

Instructions regarding War Diaries and Intelligence Summaries are contained in F. S. Regs., Part II. and the Staff Manual respectively. Title pages will be prepared in manuscript.

Place	Date	Hour	Summary of Events and Information	Remarks and references to Appendices
	September 1917.			
BETHUNE	23rd (Cont)		from 1st Fd Amb Reinfmt section. Visits by O.B.S. 1st Army	
			R Work. Appeals Borderline 8/242 hopeless and hb 1.C. train	B.G
			Sent in from A.D.C. 1 horse for treatment. Visits by O.B.S. 1st-	B.5
			Army from D.D.O.S. XI Corps and O.R.S. 2nd Div & VIIIth and Mule Pony	B.5
			Depot. 8 animals from no 1 Fd Amb Reinfmt section	3 ezly
			R Work. Eventuals VI b animals hopeless	
			Visits here. two officers hope hosp 1.C. train	
			1 Remount at hb 1 F.C. and referrals one - stallion	
			of dull nature. Towards 2 Restore from hb St. Vern	

WAR DIARY or INTELLIGENCE SUMMARY

Army Form C. 2118.

Place	Date	Hour	Summary of Events and Information	Remarks and references to Appendices
BETHUNE	October 1917		Ride with units Punctures of 6" Lule Ambulances and No 2 [illegible handwritten entries]	

WAR DIARY
or
INTELLIGENCE SUMMARY
(Erase heading not required.)

Army Form C. 2118

Place	Date	Hour	Summary of Events and Information	Remarks and references to Appendices
La Fontenelle Farm	Oct 7		Capt A.R.B. Richman proceeds on leave to Canada. Capt J. Dunlop A.V.C. took over command of this unit. The section moved from Bethune to La Fontenelle Farm.	
"	8		Routine work. Erection of shelters and stabling for horses.	
"	9		Continued work of improving conditions. Arrangements with proprietor of farm. Use of cow sheds for horses.	
"	10		Routine work. Formed a segregation hospital for ophthalmia cases in the division. Drilts horses of 5th, 226th & 463rd Coys R.E.	
"	11		Routine work. Received several horses for treatment of ophthalmia.	
"	12		" " Evacuated 7 horses and 2 mules to base Vety Hospital	
"	13		" " Visited units of 5th Inf Bde. and examined horses	
"	14		" " Evacuated 13 horses and 9 mules to base Vety Hospital. Visited 5th, 22nd & 463rd R.E. Coys.	
"	15		Routine work. Have received several cases for treatment of ophthalmia. Visited horses of 6th Field Ambulance.	

WAR DIARY
or
INTELLIGENCE SUMMARY.
(Erase heading not required.)

Army Form C. 2118.

Place	Date	Hour	Summary of Events and Information	Remarks and references to Appendices
La Fontenelle Farm	Oct 16		Routine Work. 7 men arrived from No 4 Vety Hospital to replace 7 "Category A" men at present with the Section.	By Evening Ea ??
"	" 17		Routine Work. Visited units of 6th Inf Bde and inspected horses.	
"	" 18		" " " 7 men Category "A" despatched to No 2 Vety. Hospital	
"	"		Evacuated 17 horses and 3 mules	
"	" 19		Routine Work. Inspected Saddlery & rifles of Section. Visited S.T.T. 226 CT	
"	"		and 483rd Coys. R.E.	
"	" 20		Routine Work. Visited 6 Field Ambulance & respirator issues.	
"	" 21		" " Visited units of 5th Inf. Bde. and examined S horses.	
"	" 22		" " Inspected gas-helmets of section	
"	" 23		" " Visited S.T.T., 226th CT, 483rd Coys R.E. & ??	
"	"		inspected horses and mules	
"	" 24		Routine work. The personnel of the section, has bore respirators -	
"	"		tested and passed through gas chamber at Lethonnum.	
"	" 25		Routine work.	
"	" 26		" "	

WAR DIARY
or
INTELLIGENCE SUMMARY.
(Erase heading not required.)

Army Form C. 2118.

Place	Date	Hour	Summary of Events and Information	Remarks and references to Appendices
La Fontenelle	Oct 27		Routine work. Rifle and saddling inspection. Horse sent to Amer to fetch 4	
Laire	28		Came from D 48th Bg.	
			Routine work. Visits and inspects horses of the Three Engineer units viz 3rd	
			326th and 4 Bus Field Cops.	
	29		Routine Work. Visits & inspects horses of 6th Field Ambulance	
	30		" "	
	31		" " Visits by D.A.D.V.S. who inspects Ophthalmia cases. All	
			cases progressing satisfactorily and four returned to work.	

Army Form C. 2118.

WAR DIARY
or
INTELLIGENCE SUMMARY.
(Erase heading not required.)

No. 3 M.V.S.   M 38

Instructions regarding War Diaries and Intelligence Summaries are contained in F.S. Regs., Part II. and the Staff Manual respectively. Title pages will be prepared in manuscript.

Place	Date	Hour	Summary of Events and Information	Remarks and references to Appendices
Lebucquiere	November 1		Routine work	
"	2		"	
"	3		"	
"	4		"	
"	5		Left Lebucquiere; proceeds by road to Bus	
Busnes	6		" " " " " Merville	
Merville	7		" " " " " Eecke	
Eecke	8		" " " " " Vau Hergeele	
Hergeele	9		Routine Work	
"	10		Left Hergeele; proceeds by road to Wormhoudt	
Wormhoudt	11, 16, 23, 24		Routine Work.	
"			Left Wormhoudt; proceeds by road to Esquelbeq; entrained thus along with 1 Coy 1st KRR's and the 100th Field Ambulance.	
Bapaume	25		Detrained at Achiet le grand & proceeds to Bapaume	

T2134. Wt. W708—776. 500000. 4/15. Sir J. C. & S.

WAR DIARY
or
INTELLIGENCE SUMMARY.
(Erase heading not required.)

No 3 M.V.S. (continued)

Army Form C. 2118.

Place	Date	Hour	Summary of Events and Information	Remarks and references to Appendices
Bapaume	November			
	25		Routine Work.	
	26			
	27			
	28		Left Bapaume, proceeded to N°2 Central near Edgecourt and bilited over 4th Corps Veterinary Convalescent Clearing Station from 48th M.V.S.	
	29			
	30		Routine work.	

Henry Carson
No 3. M.V.S.
O.C.

D.A.G.,
G.H.Q.,
3rd Echelon.

    Herewith War Diary of No.3 Mobile Veterinary Section for 1st to 22nd December, 1917.

    The delay in rendering this portion of the Diary is due to O.C., No.3 M.V.S. having been on leave to the United Kingdom.

                                   2/Lieut.,

H.Q., 2nd Divn.   for Major-General,
14/1/18.   Commanding 2nd Division.

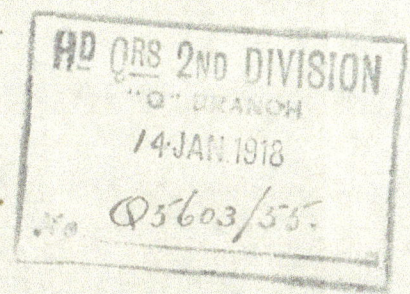

WAR DIARY or INTELLIGENCE SUMMARY

Army Form C. 2118.

Vol 39

No 3 M.V.S.

Place	Date	Hour	Summary of Events and Information	Remarks and references to Appendices
Beirut Factory	February 1917			
Ethiopia	1	22	Routine Work. The section acting as Corps Veterinary Casualty Clearing station. On 23rd Capt. Og. Wachel A.V.C. took over command of the unit, Capt. J. Dunlop A.V.C. proceeding on leave.	99 Dunlop Capt-A.V.C. O.C. 3rd M.V.S.

WAR DIARY
or
INTELLIGENCE SUMMARY.
(Erase heading not required.)

No 3 M.V.S
2nd Div

Army Form C. 2118.

Instructions regarding War Diaries and Intelligence Summaries are contained in F. S. Regs., Part II. and the Staff Manual respectively. Title pages will be prepared in manuscript.

Place	Date	Hour	Summary of Events and Information	Remarks and references to Appendices
Bellfoot Factory	DEC. 23		Took over command of No 3 MVS (acting as 5th Corps CCS) from Capt Dunlop A.V.C. who proceeded on leave. Routine work of Section.	Section Capt A.V.C. No 3 M.V.S
ETRICOURT	24		Routine work of Section. D.A.V.S. visited Section. Inspected Sick. (Officer of Train)	
	25		Routine work of Section. Evacuated 195 animals to No 7 Vet. Hospital after worn. holiday.	
	26		Routine work of Section. A.D.V.S. visited Section. Leucing mange suspected.	
	27		Routine work of Section. Inspected billet- tooth sore.	
	28		Routine work of Section. 89 animals (82 horses & 7 mules) to No 7 Vet Hospital. Saddlery & Rifle inspection - 1 NCO & 3 men attached from 53 D MVS for duty	
	29		Routine work of Section. Inspected Ooh. lame Horse.	
	30 31		Routine work of Section. Routine work of Section. Inspected Vet tub well - Gas masks.	
	JAN. 1		Routine	

Army Form C. 2118.

WAR DIARY
or
INTELLIGENCE SUMMARY.
(Erase heading not required.)

3 Mot Vety See
Vol 4 No

Place	Date	Hour	Summary of Events and Information	Remarks and references to Appendices
(Beelfoot) (poetry) ETRICOURT	JAN 1918			
	1		Routine worth of Fectin - Gracualia 14 animals to No 7 Vet Hosp	
	2		6 to No 5 Vet hosp. On completion of duty with No 3 MVS. ADVS wolia Section. 1e Constructor of "Maupe dips".	
	2		Routine worth of Section. 2 men from No 2 Vet Hosp joined Section for duty.	
	3		Routine worth of Section - Inspection- billets, cook house etc.	
	4		Routine worth of Section - Gracualia 81 horses, 3 mules to No 7 Vet hospital -	
	5		Routine worth of Section. General fatigues -	
	6		Routine worth of Section. 2 men joined Section from No 2 Vet hospital. Saddlery & rifle inspection -	
	7		Routine worth of Section. Inspected billets, cook house -	
	8		Routine worth of Section. General fatigues.	
	9		Routine worth of Section.	
	10		Routine worth of Section. ADVS visited Section by	
	11		Routine worth of Section. 210 horses & 24 mules pack quied train to No 4 Vet Hospital	
	12		Routine worth of Section. Salved Saddlery. hand steer horses, tricks left by cavalry -	
	13		Routine worth of Section -	

Fraser Capt A.I.
No 3 MVS

Army Form C. 2118.

WAR DIARY
or
INTELLIGENCE SUMMARY.
(Erase heading not required.)

No. 3 M.V.S.

Place	Date	Hour	Summary of Events and Information	Remarks and references to Appendices
Buline Factory				
Etricourt	Jan 12		Capt J James Cp AVC returns from leave. Capt J Walsh AVC returns to 41st Bde. R.F.A.	
	14		Routine Work. The unit continues to act as a Vet. Casualty Clearing Station for V Corps. Since commencing in that capacity	
	31		over 3000 animals have been evacuated to Base hospitals.	

WAR DIARY or INTELLIGENCE SUMMARY

Army Form C. 2118.

No 3 Mobile Vet. Section 2nd Div.

Vol 41

Place	Date	Hour	Summary of Events and Information	Remarks and references to Appendices
ETRICOURT	1918			
	1 Feb.		Routine work. The unit is still acting as C.C.S. for V. Corps. The site occupied is being prepared as a permanent Veterinary Evacuation Station.	
			121 Animals dispatched by rail to No 7 Vet. Hospital.	
V.2. Central	7			
	8		Routine work. Inspection of Rifles, gas helmets, harness and equipment.	
	9		" 128 Animals dispatches by rail to No 7 Vet. Hospital.	
	10		Routine work. Part of new stabling complete.	
	12		" 64 Animals dispatches by rail to No 7 Vet. Hospital.	
	13		Routine Work.	
	14		" 75 Animals dispatches to same hospital.	
	15		Routine work.	
	16			
	17		General moves. D.V.S. inspectes the unit and were accompanied by D.D.V.S. 3rd Army, A.D.V.S. V Corps, D.A.D.V.S. 2nd Division.	
	18			

Henry Cole
O.C.
M.V.S

Army Form C. 2118.

WAR DIARY
or
INTELLIGENCE SUMMARY.
(Erase heading not required.)

Instructions regarding War Diaries and Intelligence Summaries are contained in F. S. Regs., Part II. and the Staff Manual respectively. Title pages will be prepared in manuscript.

Place	Date	Hour	Summary of Events and Information	Remarks and references to Appendices
ETRICOURT	1915			
V.I. Central	Feb. 18		and two American Veterinary Officers. The visit was partly in order to give the two latter an insight in the methods of the Vet. Service in vogue at the front.	
	19-21		Routine Work. Inspection of rifles, respirators, harness + equipment.	
	22		Routine work. Evacuated 109 Animals by rail to No 7 Vet. Hospital.	
	23-25	"	"	
	26	5-6	"	
	27-28	"	V. Corps Horse clip was completed and several animals have been successfully put through today.	

Handly Coats
O.C. 3 M.V.S.

T2134. Wt. W708—776. 500000. 4/15. Sir J. C. & S.

WAR DIARY or INTELLIGENCE SUMMARY.

Army Form C. 2118.

3 M.V.S Vol 4 2nd Div

Place	Date	Hour	Summary of Events and Information	Remarks and references to Appendices
Bertrancourt Sucrerie Etrieux	March 19		Routine Work. The unit continues to act as a Veterinary Evacuating Station with additional personnel from base hospital and the M.V.S.s	
	20		The area was shelled regularly all day. Preparations to move were made.	
	21		On orders of 2nd Div. Q unit moved at 5 a.m. on 22/3/18 to Beauremont	
	22		with all attached personnel, stores, vehicles and 80 sick animals.	
Beauremont	23		2nd Div. Q was unable to give exact orders regarding moving back, but suggested La Bargue. On arrival there the tactical situation rendered another move back imperative and a verbal message was received from 2nd Div. Q to do so. Unit then moved to Meaulte.	
Meaulte	24		80 sick animals evacuated for rail from Albert. 30 remounts taken over from 2nd Army Field Remount Section. Unit moved to Vadencourt. 40 animals evacuated for rail from Puchvillers.	
Vadencourt	25		" Talmas.	
	26		"	
	28		Doullens and formed on V.E.S. there.	

O.C.
Henry Collins
Capt
E.R. V.S.

Army Form C. 2118.

WAR DIARY
or
INTELLIGENCE SUMMARY.
(Erase heading not required.)

Place	Date	Hour	Summary of Events and Information	Remarks and references to Appendices
Donllens	Nov 29		Routine work	
	30			
	31		Capt W. Herberg A.V.C. assumed command of No 5 M.V.S.	

Army Form C. 2118.

WAR DIARY
or
INTELLIGENCE SUMMARY.
(Erase heading not required.)

3 M.V.S. 2nd Div.

Place	Date	Hour	Summary of Events and Information	Remarks and references to Appendices
Viesnes	April 1		Detachment of the M.V.S. under the O.C. arrived & reported to S.A.D.V.S. remained en	
Retheuil	2		route chiefly on the following day moved to 2nd Corps Gremmevored receiving sick animals.	
"	3		34 animals evacuated to V Corps V.E.S. Flanders.	
"	4		22	
"	5		Unit moved to Dunkhen en route for Frevent. The complete unit (feet having been previously left with V Corps V.E.S.) ababu	
Dunkhen	6		off for Frevent in the morning.	
Frevent	7		A.D.V.S. X Corps requested that the unit whilst at Frevent act as X Corps V.E.S.	
	9		30 tracks (237 animals) sent off to No. 13 Vety Hospital, hay Chatel.	
	10		Continued to act as a X Corps V.E.S. Routine work	
	11		arranging standings etc. 37 other ranks moved from base hospital	
	12		V.E.S. handed over to Capt. Stevens. M.V.S moved to Coturelle.	
Coturelle	13		Routine Work	

WAR DIARY
or
INTELLIGENCE SUMMARY.
(Erase heading not required.)

3 M.V.S.   2nd Div.

Army Form C. 2118.

Place	Date	Hour	Summary of Events and Information	Remarks and references to Appendices
Authuille	April 17		Visited D.A.D.V.S. at Bavincourt. Visited the 6th Inf. Bde. animals at Saillenhout & the 10th D.C.L.I. at Bailleul-au-Bois. Called on the O.C. 6 Inf. Gds. Bde. & arranged to take over their position (Saillenhout) in the event of their moving out. Routine work.	Wilfrid Edgar, O.C. 3 M.V.S.
"	18		" " 18 animals evacuated to Abbeville.	
"	19		" "	
"	20		" "	
"	21		" "	
"	22		A.D.V.S. VI Corps. inspected the M.V.S. & expressed satisfaction. Routine work.	
"	23		" "	
"	24		" " 21 animals evacuated to Abbeville. Attended the D.A.D.V.S.'s inspection of the 6th Inf. Bde. & 10th D.C.L.I. Nothing amiss.	
"	25		Routine work. Visited Nos 2, 3 & 4 Cyc. Div. Train & found their animals both first rate as usual.	
"	26		Visited, in the afternoon, two sick horses belonging to a French peasant at Humbercourt.	
"	27		Routine work. Received instructions that probably we would soon be required to move to Bavincourt.	

WAR DIARY or INTELLIGENCE SUMMARY

Army Form C. 2118.

3 M.V.S. 2nd Echelon

Place	Date	Hour	Summary of Events and Information	Remarks and references to Appendices
Corbie	April 28		Routine work. Received notification that soon six men would can be sent to help make up the personnel of VI Corps V.E.d. at Longueau station. Since the unit came to France with the B.E.F. in 1914 care was taken to select the more recently joined men for the V.E.S. In 3 M.V.S. was mobilised (about Aug 5th 1914) & came to France about Aug 16th that year. It is noteworthy that there is an A.S.C. Driver (Lr West) who was mobilised with the M.V.S. on Aug 5th 1914 & is still a Driver with the Section. The administrative duties of the Corps are carried out by an A.D.V.S.	W. Maple Veterinary O.C. 3 M.V.S.
"	29		One truck load of sick was sent to the base as that we should have as few sick or lame as possible if required to move.	
"	30		Routine work.	

T2134. Wt. W708—776. 500000. 4/15. Sir J. C. & S.

ORIGINAL

WAR DIARY
No 3 MOBILE VETERINARY
SECTION
FOR
MAY 1918

CONFIDENTIAL

Army Form C. 2118.

WAR DIARY
or
INTELLIGENCE SUMMARY.
(Erase heading not required.)

War Diary of No. 3. Mobile Vety Section

Instructions regarding War Diaries and Intelligence Summaries are contained in F. S. Regs., Part II. and the Staff Manual respectively. Title pages will be prepared in manuscript.

Place	Date	Hour	Summary of Events and Information	Remarks and references to Appendices
Port Said	24/7/16	9 AM	Disembarked from H.M.T. Jorilla. entrained commencing for Moascar camp.	
Moascar	26/7/16	6 AM	Camp arrangements being complete the section was ready to receive sick animals and several cases of Pneumonia (equine) were admitted from S.B. Bty. R.F.A.	
Moascar	30/7/16	9 AM	Army form B. 103. for all personnel which were shown or nominal well leaving Mesopotamia. A.F. B. 2/3. Field returns army form 0/8/10 part II orders, and all correspondence files relating to this section were forwarded to D.A.D.S. 3rd Echelon Indian Section, Alexandria.	
Moascar	1/8/16		Six riding horses were received from remount depot, which were of a very poor class.	
Moascar	10/8/16	9 AM	One section horse was evacuated to No. 2 Field Vety. detachment.	
Moascar	19/8/16		Five animals were admitted with colic all of which were evacuated.	
Moascar	31/7/16		Two cases of colitis and one of strangles were admitted.	

WAR DIARY
or
INTELLIGENCE SUMMARY

Army Form C. 2118.

Place	Date	Hour	Summary of Events and Information	Remarks and references to Appendices
Mosul	31/8	8 AM	O.C. proceeded on leave to Cairo. A.D.M.S. took over charge of section.	EB
	31 to 30/8		Nothing of importance to note. During the month eighty-six cases were admitted for treatment. Thirty-of which were returned cured to their units. Nine were transferred sick. Seventeen were evacuated sick to No. 3 Field Vy. detachment. Six died. One was destroyed. Twenty-three remaining under treatment. The majority of the animals admitted were in a poor condition, but others received with careful and judicious feeding. Stores rations were good. No scale of issue being laid down. Many Eby H. Bran also 2. Stay 10b. 12. Gram Fodder occasionally. The troops rations were a good percentage below the issue in Mesopotamia.	EB

TB Bennett Capture
Comdg. No. 3, Mobile Vety Station

Army Form C. 2118.

WAR DIARY
or
INTELLIGENCE SUMMARY.
(Erase heading not required.)

3 M.V.S. 2nd Div

Place	Date	Hour	Summary of Events and Information	Remarks and references to Appendices
Beaumont	May 1		Moved into Beaumont in the afternoon	
"	2		Lithlgown visited the 10th D.C.L.I. at Esbo-en-Ivon & attended at Billelment for a short time on inspection of 6th Bn/65th Transport by the D.T.O. 2nd Div.	
"	3		I visited the Div. train at Cutwell, called on the O.C. 42nd M.V.S. at Larbret. Weather greatly improved.	
	4			
	5		Osmanlike in the past two days. Mornings still wet & stormy.	
	6		Routine work.	
	7			
	8			
			Evacuated 11 horses & 3 mules by Veterinary Rail head.	
			Routine work. Not many sick animals being received.	
	12		Football team played a team from the 42nd M.V.S. Latter team won by five goals to two.	
	13		Routine work.	
	14		17 horses & 2 mules evacuated from Army Veterinary railhead.	

Army Form C. 2118.

WAR DIARY
or
INTELLIGENCE SUMMARY.
(Erase heading not required.)

3 M.V.S. 2nd Div

Instructions regarding War Diaries and Intelligence Summaries are contained in F. S. Regs., Part II. and the Staff Manual respectively. Title pages will be prepared in manuscript.

Place	Date	Hour	Summary of Events and Information	Remarks and references to Appendices
Beaumont	May 15		Routine work. Visitation of units etc.	
"	16		"	
"	17		" At night several bombs were dropped by enemy aeroplanes in the vicinity of the Section but no damage was done to this unit.	
"	18		Routine work.	
"	19		"	
"	20		"	
"	21		21 horses & 4 mules inspected via faulty nailhead.	
"	22		D.A.D.V.S. made a thorough inspection of the M.V.S. lines and sheds corps mangle.	
"	23		Reclassification of the kennels. Twenty ill "not A". 5 horses & 1 mule were via faulty nailhead to fill up one of the trucks ordered by the O.C. 42nd Mo. V.S.	
"	24		Routine work	
"	25		Orders received to send off the six men awaiting transfer to self from the Y.I. Corps of M.E.S. at Gray-en-artois. Member of Board for examination of shoeing Smith at Lealoy.	

Army Form C. 2118.

WAR DIARY
or
INTELLIGENCE SUMMARY.

3rd M.V.D. 2nd Line

(Erase heading not required.)

Place	Date	Hour	Summary of Events and Information	Remarks and references to Appendices
	May			
Beaumont	26 } 28 }		Routine work. Visitation of units.	
	29.		G.O.C. inspected the M.V.D. Special mention of the splendid condition of the horses.	
	30 } 31 }		Routine work.	

Army Form C. 2118.

WAR DIARY
or
INTELLIGENCE SUMMARY.
(Erase heading not required.)

3 M.V.S. 2nd Div

Instructions regarding War Diaries and Intelligence Summaries are contained in F. S. Regs., Part II. and the Staff Manual respectively. Title pages will be prepared in manuscript.

Place	Date	Hour	Summary of Events and Information	Remarks and references to Appendices
Buissart	June 1		Routine work of Section. Evacuated 15 Horses & 4 Mules (which included 2 Horses from American Units) to No 14 Veterinary Hosp:	
	2		Routine work of Section. One Mule (L.D.) admitted for Debility. This is not a very bad case & will be fit for issue after treatment. Also 1 (MD) Horse admitted with Broken heel for treatment. Neka very bad case & will slowly be fit for issue.	
	3		Admitted 2 animals from American Units.	
	4		Routine work. Men engaged in digging anti-bomb traverses round horse lines.	
	5		Routine work. 1 Mule (LD) received from 2nd Machine Gun Bn for treatment. This animal will be treated & returned to its Unit. — D.D.R. inspected a number of horses sent in for casting purposes. Only 3 cases were considered suitable for casting.	
	6		Routine work. Evacuated 8 Horses & 3 Mules (including 2 animals from American Units & No 3 cases "cast" by D.D.R.) to No 6 V.E.S. at GOUY-EN-ARTOIS. Visited Billet of Guards Divn: M.V.S. at HUMBERCAMP who will relieve tomorrow.	
	7		Section moved to HUMBERCAMP in relief of Guards Divn M.V.S. — Generally	

Army Form C. 2118.

WAR DIARY
or
INTELLIGENCE SUMMARY.
(Erase heading not required.)

Instructions regarding War Diaries and Intelligence Summaries are contained in F. S. Regs., Part II. and the Staff Manual respectively. Title pages will be prepared in manuscript.

Place	Date	Hour	Summary of Events and Information	Remarks and references to Appendices
HUMBERCAMP	June 7		Settling down. 1 Horse (R) from D/178 Bde RFA admitted suffering from strangles wounds. Extracted shrapnel. A bad case & will have to be evacuated.	
	8		Routine work.	
	9 (Monday)		Routine work.	
	10		Routine work. A case of suspected Mange admitted, but on examination was found not to be suffering from skin disease. This animal is debilitated & will be kept for treatment.	
	11		Routine work. 7 Horses & 2 Mules evacuated to No 6 V.E.S. A 20 horse from H.Q. Bty RHA admitted yesterday with fractured ulna destroyed as it was a hopeless case. Horse from D/181 Bde RFA with wounds contused admitted for treatment.	
	12		Routine work. Horse received a few days ago from 1st KRRs with sprain. No horses cured & issued to M.M.P.s	
	13		Routine work. A very bad case of Mange received from A 181 Bde RFA.	
	14		Routine work. Evacuated 7 Horses & 1 Mule to No 6 V.E.S.	
	15		Routine work & general fatigues	

Army Form C. 2118.

WAR DIARY
or
INTELLIGENCE SUMMARY.
(Erase heading not required.)

Instructions regarding War Diaries and Intelligence Summaries are contained in F.S. Regs., Part II. and the Staff Manual respectively. Title pages will be prepared in manuscript.

Place	Date	Hour	Summary of Events and Information	Remarks and references to Appendices
HUMBERCAMP	June 16 (Sunday)		Routine work. 1 Horse admitted from 23rd Ryl Fusiliers with wound in hip for treatment.	
	17		Routine work. Evacuated 5 Horses to No. 6 V.E.S.	
	18		Routine work. Evacuated 7 Horses to No. 6 V.E.S.	
	19		Routine work. New anti-bomb traverses nearing completion	
	20		Routine work. Evacuated 5 Horses & 1 Mule to No. 6 V.E.S.	
	21		Routine work & general fatigues. 2 Animals admitted for treatment and returned to unit.	
	22		Routine work. Evacuated 8 Horses to No. 6 V.E.S.	
	23		Routine work. Anti-bomb traverses completed & prickling line erected.	
	24		Routine work. Evacuated 4 Horses & 1 Mule to No. 6 V.E.S.	
	25		Routine work. Evacuated 4 Horses & 4 Mules to No. 6 V.E.S.	
	26		Returned from leave to Scotland. During absence DADVS has been looking after the U.V.S.	
	27		Routine work	
	28		4 horses & 4 mules evac. to No. 6 V.E.S.	
	29-30		Routine work. Visitation of units	

WAR DIARY
or
INTELLIGENCE SUMMARY.
(Erase heading not required.)

No. 3 M.V.S. 2nd Divn.

Army Form C. 2118.

Place	Date	Hour	Summary of Events and Information	Remarks and references to Appendices
HUMBERCAMP	July 1		Routine work.	
	2		Routine work. Evacuated 8 Horses & 3 Mules to No. 6 V.E.S.	
	3		Routine work	
	4		Routine work	
	5		Routine work	
	6		Routine work. Evacuated 9 Horses & 1 Mule to No. 6 V.E.S.	
	7		Routine work	
	8		Routine work – Destroyed 10 Horse suffering from Gunshot wounds N Hock	
	9		Routine work Evacuated 7 Horses & 11 Mules to No. 6 V.E.S.	
	10		Routine work.	
	11		Routine work	
	12		Routine work. Capt Harley under orders to proceed to No. 14 Veterinary Hospital – Capt J.D. Brown A.V.C. arrived in relief.	A Browne Captain OC No 3 MVS

WAR DIARY or INTELLIGENCE SUMMARY

Army Form C. 2118.

Place	Date	Hour	Summary of Events and Information	Remarks and references to Appendices
Amberieuse	July 13		Took over command of No 3 MVS from Capt. Witherley AVC. Checked Equipment Stores etc. Evacuated 7 Horses and 1 mule to No 6 VES.	Amberieuse Citerne OC No 3 MVS
	14		Routine work	
	15		Routine work. Evacuated 2 Horses and 3 mules to No 6 VES	
	16		Routine work	
	17		Routine work	
	18		Routine work. Evacuated 11 horses & 2 mules to No 6 VES.	
	19		Routine work. Destroyed I.D. horse – brand Contrick afflick (sp. fork)	
	20		Routine work. Evacuated 11 horses to No 6 VES. Sgt Poole E. AVC	
	21		Routine work	Returned to duty; from leave.
	22		Routine work	
	23.		Routine work. Evacuated 6 horses & 5 mules to No 6 VES	
	24		Do	
	25		Do Evacuated 5 Horses (Sick) and 4 Animals cast by DDR 3rd Army to No 6 VES.	

WAR DIARY
or
INTELLIGENCE SUMMARY.
(Erase heading not required.)

Army Form C. 2118.

Place	Date	Hour	Summary of Events and Information	Remarks and references to Appendices
Hunkercamp.	July 26		Routine Work. Destroyed Rides from 226 Field G.H. 2nd Div. P.M. revealed Calculus of Small Intestines. Incinerated 8 Horses and 1 Mule G.No 6 V.E.S.	
	27		Do	
	28		Do	
	29		Do	
	30		Do Evacuated 8 Horses G No. 6 V.E.S.	
	31		Do H.D Horse admitted from 2nd Batt, 319 Inf.Bde, 80th Div. U.S.A for evacuation.	

Army Form C. 2118.

WAR DIARY
or
INTELLIGENCE SUMMARY.
(Erase heading not required.)

No. 3 M.V.S.
2nd Divn

Moore Capt R.E.
OC No 3 MVS

Place	Date	Hour	Summary of Events and Information	Remarks and references to Appendices
HUMBERCAMP	August 1		Routine work. Evacuated 9 Horses (including 1 from American Unit) to No 6 V.E.S.	
	2		1 Horse (LD) suffering from Ophthalmia cured & issued today	
	3		Routine work.	
	4		Routine work. Evacuated 6 Horses (including 3 from American Units) to No 6 V.E.S.	
	5		Routine work	
	6		Routine work. Evacuated 11 Horses & 2 Mules (including 1 Horse & 2 Mules from American Units & 1 Brood Mare from 117th Bty. 41st Bde R.F.A.) to No 6 V.E.S.	
	7		Routine work	
	8		Routine work. Evacuated 4 Horses & 2 Mules to No 6. V.E.S.	
	9		Routine work	
	10		Routine work. Evacuated 9 Horses & 3 Mules to No 6 V.E.S.	
	11			
	12		Routine work	
	13		Routine work. Evacuated 10 Horses & 1 Mule (including 1 Horse & 1 Mule from American Units) - 1 Horse (LD) from 2nd Bn Machine Gun Corps, suffering	

Army Form C. 2118.

WAR DIARY
or
INTELLIGENCE SUMMARY.
(Erase heading not required.)

Instructions regarding War Diaries and Intelligence Summaries are contained in F.S. Regs., Part II. and the Staff Manual respectively. Title pages will be prepared in manuscript.

Place	Date	Hour	Summary of Events and Information	Remarks and references to Appendices
HUMBERCAMP	Aug. 13		1 Horse (H.D.) from No 1 by 2nd Silt Train suffering from Tetanus, destroyed today.	
	14		Routine work.	
	15		Routine work. Evacuated 6 Horses & 5 Mules to No 6 V.E.S.	
	16		Routine work.	
	17		Routine work. Evacuated 11 Horses & 3 Mules (including 2 Horses from American Unit) to No 6 V.E.S.	
	18		Routine work.	
	19		Routine work. Evacuated 12 Horses & 3 Mules (including 2 Horses from American Unit) to No 6 V.E.S. Horse belonging to C.R.E. 2nd 5th (W.) lacerated N. Heel) cured & returned today.	
	20		Routine work. Evacuated 6 Horses & 1 Mule (including 1 Horse from American Unit) to No 6 V.E.S. - Advanced Veterinary Aid Post opened today at MONCHY. - 1 Horse (C.O) Arthritis (Knee joint) from HQ1st By 14th (Army) Bde R.F.A. destroyed today.	
	21		Routine work.	
	22		Routine work. Evacuated 8 Horses & 2 Mules (including 1 Horse & 1 Mule from American Units) to No 6 V.E.S.	

T2134. Wt. W708—776. 500000. 4/15. Sir J. C. & S.

WAR DIARY
or
INTELLIGENCE SUMMARY.
(Erase heading not required.)

Army Form C. 2118.

Place	Date	Hour	Summary of Events and Information	Remarks and references to Appendices
HUMBERCAMP	Aug 23		Routine work.	
	24		Routine work. Evacuated 17 Horses & 8 Mules to No. 6 V.E.S.	
	25		Routine work.	
	26		Routine work. Advanced Veterinary Aid Post moved today to DOUCHY.	
	27		Routine work.	
	28		No. 3 M.V.S. moved today to POMMIER	
POMMIER	29		Routine work. Evacuated 31 Horses & 7 Mules to No. 6 V.E.S.	
	30		Routine work.	
	31		Routine work. Evacuated 7 Horses & 1 Mule to No. 6 V.E.S.	

WAR DIARY
or
INTELLIGENCE SUMMARY.
(Erase heading not required.)

Army Form C. 2118.

No. 3 M.V.S. 2nd Div.

Vol 48

Place	Date	Hour	Summary of Events and Information	Remarks and references to Appendices
	1918 Sept.			
POMMIER	1		Routine work. Evacuated 10 Horses & 1 mule to No. 6 V.E.S.	
	2		Section moved from POMMIER to DOUCHY. Advanced Veterinary Aid Post moved to ERVILLERS	
DOUCHY	3	Do.	Evacuated 9 Horses & 2 mules to No. 6 V.E.S. Section moved to ERVILLERS.	
ERVILLERS	4	Do.	Advanced Post moved to VRAUCOURT	
	5		Section moved to MORY	
MORY	6	Do.	Evacuated 9 Horses & 2 mules to No. 6 V.E.S.	
	7	Do.	2 L.D. Horses captured from enemy, received from 2nd H.L.I. In mallenius. Negative result. L.D. Horse from 2nd Batt. M.G.C. died from Gunshot wound (Shell).	
"	8	Do.	Evacuated 9 Horses & 5 mules to No. 6 V.E.S. Rider from 2nd South Staffs destroyed for wounds Gunshot Shell.	Stborne Capt & O.C. No 3 M.V.S
"	9	Do.	2 L.D. and 1 R. captured from enemy, received from 24th Royal Fusiliers for mallenius. Negative result. Evacuated 8 Horses & 1 mule to No. 6 V.E.S.	

WAR DIARY
or
INTELLIGENCE SUMMARY.

No. 3 M.V.S.
2nd Div

Army Form C. 2118.

Place	Date	Hour	Summary of Events and Information	Remarks and references to Appendices
	1918			
MORY	Sept 10		Routine work. Advanced Veterinary Aid Post moved to MORCHIES	Melbourne Capt O/C OC No. 3 MVS
	11		Do. Evacuated 12 Horses & 3 Mules to No 6 VES	
	12		Do. Evacuated 14 Horses & 4 Mules to No 6 VES	
	13		Do. Evacuated 9 Horses & 1 Mule to No 6 VES	
	14		Do. 2 LD Horses destroyed – wounds Gunshot Shell	
			Evacuated 9 Horses & 2 Mules S/Wes, LD Mule wounded Gunshot Shell, destroyed.	
	15		Do.	
	16		Do. Evacuated 20 Horses & 4 Mules to No 6 VES	
	17		Do. Evacuated 11 Horses to No 6 VES. Charger from CRA 2nd Div destroyed on Arthritis, fetlock NF	
	18		Do. Advanced Post withdrawn	
	19		Do.	
	20		Do.	
	21		Do. Evacuated 16 Horses to No 6 VES	
	22		Do.	

Army Form C. 2118.

WAR DIARY
or
INTELLIGENCE SUMMARY.

No. 3 M.V.S. 2nd Div.

(Erase heading not required.)

Place	Date	Hour	Summary of Events and Information	Remarks and references to Appendices
	1918			
MORY.	Sept 23		Routine work.	
	24		Do. Evacuated 9 Horses & 2 Mules to No 6 V.E.S.	
	25		Do. Evacuated 13 Horses to No. 6 V.E.S.	
	26.		Do. Advanced Post established at MORCHIES	
	27.		Do.	
	28		Do. Evacuated 11 Horses & 1 Mule to No 6 V.E.S. Section moved to MORCHIES. Advanced Post moved to DOIGNIES.	
	29.		Do. Evacuated 2 Horses & 1 Mule. Section moved to DOIGNIES. Advanced Post moved to HAVRINCOURT	
	30.		Do. Evacuated 5 Horses to No 6 V.E.S. H.D Horse destroyed to wounds Gunshot Shell. Section moved to near HAVRINCOURT. Advanced Post moved to FLESQUIERES	A/Browne Capt a/c OC No. 3 M.V.S

Army Form C.2118.

No.3 M.V.S.
2nd Div.

WAR DIARY
or
INTELLIGENCE SUMMARY.
(Erase heading not required.)

Instructions regarding War Diaries and Intelligence Summaries are contained in F. S. Regs., Part II. and the Staff Manual respectively. Title pages will be prepared in manuscript.

Place	Date	Hour	Summary of Events and Information	Remarks and references to Appendices
	1918			
HAVRINCOURT	Oct. 1		Routine work	
	2		Do.	
	3		Section moved to Ribecourt. Evacuated 7 Horses & 3 Mules to No. 6 V.E.S. L.D. Horse found captured, debility, destroyed. Advanced Post recalled.	
RIBECOURT	4		Evacuated 11 Horses & 2 Mules to No. 6 V.E.S.	
	5		Do.	
	6		Evacuated 14 Horses & 6 Mules to No. 6 V.E.S.	
	7		Do.	
	8		Evacuated 14 Horses to No. 6 V.E.S. L.D. Horse from 36 Bde HQ RFA destroyed — wound Gunshot shell at 41st Bde R.F.A. Advanced Post opened at DOIGNIES. Section moved back to DOIGNIES.	
DOIGNIES	9		Evacuated 16 Horses & 2 Mules to No. 6 V.E.S.	
	10		Do.	
	11		Do.	
	12		Advanced Post recalled.	

T2134. Wt. W708—776. 500000. 4/15. Sir J. C. & S.

WAR DIARY
or
INTELLIGENCE SUMMARY.
(Erase heading not required.)

Army Form C. 2118

No. 3 M.V.S. 2nd Sect.

Place	Date	Hour	Summary of Events and Information	Remarks and references to Appendices
	1918. Oct. 13		Section moved to NOYELLES including one LD "found Captured"	
NOYELLES	14		Routine work	
	15		Do. Evacuated 8 Horses & 1 mule to No 6 V.E.S.	
	16		Do. Evacuated 10 Horses to No. 6 V.E.S. LD. Horse from 16th Batt? 4th Bde Art'a W/Sgmt? Shell destroyed	
	17		Do. Evacuated 8 Horses to No 6 V.E.S.	
	18		Do. Evacuated 6 Horses & 2 mules to No. 6 V.E.S.	
	19		Do.	
	20		Do. Section moved to IGNIEL.	
IGNIEL	21		Do.	
	22		Do. Evacuated 4 Horses & 1 mule to No. 6 V.E.S.	
	23		Do. Moved Section to St HILAIRE.	
St HILAIRE	24		Do.	
	25		Do. Evacuated 4 Horses & 1 mule to No. 6 V.E.S.	
	26		Do. Advanced Post opened with 99th Inf Bde Sect'n	

WAR DIARY
or
INTELLIGENCE SUMMARY.

(Erase heading not required.)

Army Form C. 2118.

No. 3 M V S
Indian

Place	Date	Hour	Summary of Events and Information	Remarks and references to Appendices
	1918			
St. Hilaire	Oct. 26		Routine work.	
	27		Do. Dismounted 8 Horses to No 6 VES	2 Lt
	28		Do. Evacuated 7 Horses & 2 mules to No 6 VES	21/2/0 OC No 3 VS
	29		Do. Rider from H.Q. 36 Bde RFA destroyed at Animal Post to Tetanus	
	30		Do. Evacuated 6 Horses & 3 mules to No 6 VES	
	31		Do.	

WAR DIARY
or
INTELLIGENCE SUMMARY.
(Erase heading not required.)

Army Form C. 2118.

No 3 M.V.S. 2nd Div

Place	Date	Hour	Summary of Events and Information	Remarks and references to Appendices
	1918 Nov. 1		Routine work	
St. Hilaire	1		Routine work. Evacuated 10 Horses & 1 mule to No 6 V.E.S.	
	2		Do	
	3		Do Evacuated 16 Horses & 1 mule to No 6 V.E.S. 1 H.O from 63rd Bde. R.G.A. and 1 H from 130 B.H.F. 40 Bde. 3rd Div. died (also Jaundice)	
	4		Do Evac'd 9 Horses & 2 mules to No 6 V.E.S.	
	5		Do Evac'd 7 Horses to No 6 V.E.S. Section moved to VERTAIN.	
VERTAIN	6		Do Evac'd 4 Horses & 2 mules to No 6 V.E.S.	
	7		Do Evac'd 5 Horses & 5 mules to No 6 V.E.S.	
	8		Do	
	9		Do	
	10		Do Evac'd 1 Horse & 2 mules to No 6 V.E.S. Section moved to VILLERS POL.	
Villers Pol	11		Do Evac'd 2 Horses to No 6 V.E.S.	
	12		Do Evac'd 1 Horse to No 6 V.E.S.	
	13		Do Evac'd 22 Horses & 2 mules to No 4 V.E.S.	

Army Form C. 2118.

WAR DIARY
or
INTELLIGENCE SUMMARY.
(Erase heading not required.)

No. 3 M.V.S.
2nd Arm.

Place	Date	Hour	Summary of Events and Information	Remarks and references to Appendices
	1918			
VILLERS POL	Nov 14		Routine Work. Evacuated 13 Horses & 5 Mules to No 4 V.E.S.	
	15		Do. Evacuated 17 Horses to No 4 V.E.S.	
	16		Do. Evacuated 21 Horses & 2 Mules to No 4 V.E.S.	
	17		Do. Evacuated 28 Horses & 9 Mules to No 4 V.E.S.	
	18		Do. Evacuated 17 Horses to No 4 V.E.S.	
MECQUEGNIES	19		Do. Section moved to MECQUÉGNIES.	
	20		Do. Section moved to MAUBEUGE.	
MAUBEUGE	21		Do. Transferred 6 Horses to No 19 M.V.S.	
	22		Do. Do 4 Do	
	23		Do. Do 6 Do	
	24		Do. Section moved to HAULCHIN.	
HAULCHIN	25		Do. Section moved to FONTAINE L'ÉVÊQUE	
FONTAINE L'ÉVÊQUE	26		Do.	
	27		Do. Evacuated 4 Horses to No 6 V.E.S.	
	28		Do.	

Army Form C. 2118.

WAR DIARY
or
INTELLIGENCE SUMMARY.
(Erase heading not required.)

No 3 MVS 2nd Div.

Place	Date	Hour	Summary of Events and Information	Remarks and references to Appendices
	1918			Albrune Cottage OC No 3M.V.S
Fontaine L'Evêque	Nov 29		Section moved to SART EUSTACHE.	
Sart Eustache	30		Routine work.	

Army Form C. 2118.

WAR DIARY
or
INTELLIGENCE SUMMARY.
(Erase heading not required.)

No 3 M.V.S
2nd Divn

Place	Date 1918	Hour	Summary of Events and Information	Remarks and references to Appendices
SART EUSTACHE	Dec 1		Routine work	
	2		Do	
	3		Do	
WEPION	4		Section moved to WEPION	
THON	5		Section moved to THON	
HUY	6		Section moved to HUY.	
OUFFET	7		Section moved to OUFFET. 3 Horses (40) destroyed & carcases sold to Butcher.	
CAMBLAIN LA TOUR	8		Section moved to CAMBLAIN LA TOUR	
VERT BOISSON	9		Section moved to VERT BOISSON	
	10		Routine work & general clean up.	
	11		Section moved to STER	
STER	12		Section moved to LAGER ELSENBARN - Evacuated 8 Horses & 1 Mule to No 6 V.E.S.	
LAGER ELSENBARN	13		Section moved to WITZERETH.	
WITZERETH	14		Section moved to WINDEN.	

WAR DIARY
or
INTELLIGENCE SUMMARY.
(Erase heading not required.)

No 3 M.V.S. 2nd Divn

Army Form C. 2118.

Place	Date 1918	Hour	Summary of Events and Information	Remarks and references to Appendices
WINDEN	Dec. 15		Routine work	
	16			
	17			
	18			
	19		Section moved to OBERZIER	
OBERZIER	20		Routine work	
	21		Do	1 Horse from No 2 Coy. 2nd Divt Train died – (Icaleculus)
	22		Do	1 Horse (LO) destroyed & carcase sold to Butcher
	23		Do	1 Horse (HD) destroyed & carcase sold to Butcher. Section moved to BICKESDORF.
	24		Do	
	25		Xmas day – General holiday	
BICKESDORF	26		Routine work	
	27		Do	
	28		Do	1 Mule destroyed & carcase sold to Butcher. Capt J.E. Young R.A.V.C. took over command of No 3 M.V.S., in relief of Capt J.D. Broome R.A.V.C. who proceeded to U.K. on leave

J.E. Young Capt
O/C 3 M.V.S

WAR DIARY
or
INTELLIGENCE SUMMARY.
(Erase heading not required.)

No. 3 M.V.S.
2nd Division

Army Form C. 2118.

Instructions regarding War Diaries and Intelligence Summaries are contained in F. S. Regs., Part II. and the Staff Manual respectively. Title pages will be prepared in manuscript.

Place	Date	Hour	Summary of Events and Information	Remarks and references to Appendices
	1918			
BICKESDORF	Dec 29		Routine work	
	30			
	31			

2 DIV TROOPS

3 MOB. VET. SECT

1919 JAN - 1919 OCT

Box 1013.

WAR DIARY or INTELLIGENCE SUMMARY

Army Form C. 2118.

No 3 MVS 2nd Dist

Vol 5 3

Absence Certificate OC No 3 MVS

Place	Date	Hour	Summary of Events and Information	Remarks and references to Appendices
	1919			
Bishopton	Jan 1		Rankins Work	
	2		One HD horse from 1/ Kent H.B. Paraplegia, destroyed for knackery purposes	
	3		Do	
	4		Do One HB horse from 127 HB. Ulc Cellulitis "	
	5		Do	
	6		Do Evacuated 13 Horses to No 6 V.E.S. One HD horse from 2nd Section, 2nd DAC, ulc Cellulitis, destroyed for knackery purposes	
	7		Do	
	8		Do	
	9		Do One HB horse from 1/ Kent HB. Ulc Cellulitis, destroyed for knackery purposes	
	10		Do	
	11		Do	
	12		Do Evacuated 39 Horses & 3 mules to No 6 V.E.S.	
	13		Do	
	14		Do	
	15		Do Evacuated 4 Horses to No 6 V.E.S.	

Army Form C. 2118.

WAR DIARY
or
INTELLIGENCE SUMMARY.

(Erase heading not required.)

No. 3 MVS
2nd Division

Place	Date	Hour	Summary of Events and Information	Remarks and references to Appendices
Ritschoff	Jan 16 1919		Routine work. One LD horse from D/361 Bde? 36 Bde RFA 2nd Div, W.o Colachilli and one LD horse from C/34 Bde a.Sh pshills, destroyed for butchery purposes.	Albuera Catt. Regt No 5
	17	do		
	18	do		
	19	do		
	20	do		
	21	do	Evacuated 76 Horses & 9 mules to No 6 V.E.S.	
	22	do	Evacuated 8 Horses to No 6 V.E.S.	
	23	do		
	24	do		
	25	do	Evacuated 4 Horses to No 6 V.E.S.	
	26	do		
	27	do	Evacuated 6 Horses & 4 mules to No 6 V.E.S. One LD horse from 2nd Signal Co RE, Calahese, destroyed for butchery purposes.	
	28	do	One Reserve horse Belgian mariner 2nd Div, brand burned OT and one LD horse from SdA Gosh 2nd RAC dislocation Patella, destroyed for butchery purposes.	

WAR DIARY
or
INTELLIGENCE SUMMARY.
(Erase heading not required.)

Army Form C. 2118.

No 3 MVS
2nd Division.

Place	Date	Hour	Summary of Events and Information	Remarks and references to Appendices
Reikedorp/Jun	1919 28		Routine work. One Pony from S.a.a Sec, 2nd DAC heavily Dermatitis, destroyed for butchery purposes.	Absence Capt & OC No 3 MVS
	29		Do. Evacuated 14 Horses & 1 Mule to No 6 V.E.S.	
	30		Do.	
	31		Do. Evacuated 6 Horses & 2 Mules to No 6 V.E.S.	

WAR DIARY
or
INTELLIGENCE SUMMARY.
(Erase heading not required.)

Army Form C. 2118.

No 3 M.V.S.
2nd Division

9/II 54

Place	Date	Hour	Summary of Events and Information	Remarks and references to Appendices
Bukandry	1919. Feb. 1		Routine work. L.D. Horse from 2 Sektn, 2nd DAC, Ulcerative Cellulitis, destroyed for butchery purposes.	
	2		Do	
	3		Do	
	4		Do	
	5		Do	
	6		Do	
	7		Do	
	8		Do	
	9		Do	
	10		Do	
	11		Do	
	12		Do	
	13		Do	
	14		Do	
	15		Do. L.D. Horse from 48/304, 36 Bde RFA (Wound cont. kick) destroyed for butchery purposes. H.D. " No 1 Co. 7, 2nd Div Train, Calculus	

A.Brown Capt. R.A.V.C.
O.C. 3 M.V.S

WAR DIARY or INTELLIGENCE SUMMARY

No 3 MVS 2nd Division

Army Form C. 2118

Place	Date	Hour	Summary of Events and Information	Remarks and references to Appendices
Birkendorf	1919 Feb. 16		Routine Work. Evacuated 2 Horses & 1 mule to No 6 V.E.S.	
	17		Do	
	18		Do Evacuated 29 Horses & 4 mules to No 6 V.E.S. H.D. horse from 129 Heavy Batt? R.G.A. Debility, destroyed for butchery purposes.	
	19		Do	
	20		Do LD mule from 71 Batt? 36 Bde R.F.A. Stomach Cont. kick, destroyed for butchery purposes.	
	21		Do	
	22		Do Evacuated 7 Horses	
	23		Do	
	24		Do Evacuated 20 Horses & 10 mules 6 No.6 V.E.S. This total includes 18 D and 9 D- cases.	
	25		Do LD Horse from S.A.A. Sect 2nd Bde, Colic(?), destroyed for butchery purposes	
	26		Do	
	27		Do	
	28		Do Evacuated 2 Horses 6 No.6 V.E.S. This total includes 1 D Case. LD Horse from D 36 Bty, 36 Bde R.F.A Laminitis, destroyed for butchery purposes. H.D. from 14 Heavy Batt? R.G.A. Picked up nail	A.Browne 2/Lt R.A.V.C. O.C. No 3 M.V.S.

Army Form C. 2118.

WAR DIARY
or
INTELLIGENCE SUMMARY.
(Erase heading not required.)

No 3 M.V.S. Light Div.

Place	Date	Hour	Summary of Events and Information	Remarks and references to Appendices
BIRKESDORF	1919 March 1st		Routine work	
	2nd			
	3rd			
	4th			
	5th		Routine work. Evacuated 7 Horses & 4 Mules to No 6 V.E.S – 1 Animal destroyed 4 sold for Butchery purposes for Mks 700.	
	6th		Routine work. 1 Animal destroyed & sold for Butchery purposes for Mks 900	
	7th		Routine work.	
	8th		Routine work	
	9th		Routine work. Evacuated 9 Horses to No 6 V.E.S.	
	10th		Routine work	
	11th		Routine work. Evacuated 17 Horses to No 6 V.E.S.	
	12th		Routine work. Evacuated 3 Horses to No 6 V.E.S.	
	13th		Routine work. 2 Animals destroyed & sold for Butchery purposes for Mks 1300	
	14th		Routine work. 4 Animals destroyed & sold for Butchery purposes for Mks 2800	
	15th		Routine work	

Army Form C. 2118.

WAR DIARY
or
INTELLIGENCE SUMMARY.
(Erase heading not required.)

No. 3 M.V.S. Light Division

Instructions regarding War Diaries and Intelligence Summaries are contained in F.S. Regs., Part II. and the Staff Manual respectively. Title pages will be prepared in manuscript.

Place	Date	Hour	Summary of Events and Information	Remarks and references to Appendices
BIRKESDORF	1919 March 16th		Routine work	W. Erickson Capt. O.C. No.3 M.V.S.
	17th		Routine work	
	18th		Routine work	
	19th		Routine work	
	20th		Routine work	
	21st		Routine work. Evacuated 13 Horses & 6 Mules to No 6 V.E.S. – 14 Animals destroyed & sold for Butchery purposes for Mks 12000	
	22nd		Routine work	
	23rd		Routine work	
	24th		Routine work. 1 Animal destroyed & sold for Butchery purposes for Mks 900	
	25th		Routine work. Command of No 3 M.V.S. taken over by Capt G. WAGHER R.A.V.C. vice Capt J.D. BROOKE R.A.V.C. (demobilized)	
	26th		Routine work. 7 Horses & 1 Mule evacuated to No 4 V.E.S. – 3 Animals destroyed & sold for Butchery purposes for Mks 1100	
	27th		Routine work	
	28th		Routine work	
	29th		Routine work. Evacuate 4 Horses to No 4 V.E.S. – 2 N.C.O.'s 4 men proceeded to 2nd Army Concentration Camp for dispersal.	

Army Form C. 2118.

WAR DIARY
or
INTELLIGENCE SUMMARY.
(Erase heading not required.)

No 3 M.V.S. Night Divn

Instructions regarding War Diaries and Intelligence Summaries are contained in F. S. Regs., Part II. and the Staff Manual respectively. Title pages will be prepared in manuscript.

Place	Date	Hour	Summary of Events and Information	Remarks and references to Appendices
BARTEESDORF	1919 March 30		Routine work	
	31st		Routine work. Evacuated 5 Horses to No A.V.E.S.	

W Thinkwer CyhAVC No 3 M.V.S.

Army Form C. 2118.

WAR DIARY
or
INTELLIGENCE SUMMARY.
(Erase heading not required.)

No 314 V.S. Light Division

Instructions regarding War Diaries and Intelligence Summaries are contained in F. S. Regs., Part II. and the Staff Manual respectively. Title pages will be prepared in manuscript.

Place	Date	Hour	Summary of Events and Information	Remarks and references to Appendices
BIRKESDORF	1919 Jan. 1		Routine work	2.7.0
	2		Routine work. 2 men reported for duty with No 314 V.S.	2.7.0
	3		Routine work. Evacuated 6 Horses & 2 Mules to No 4 V.E.S. - 1 Mule from No 1 V.E.S. destroyed by D.A.C. for Butchery purposes	2.7.0
	4		Routine work. No 1 Section Light D.A.C. destroyed 2 cats for Butchery purposes. Evacuated 8 Horses to No 4 V.E.S. - 1 Mule from S.A.A. Section Light D.A.C. destroyed & sold for Butchery purposes	2.7.0
	5		Routine work. Evacuated 1 Horse & 3 Mules to No 4 V.E.S.	2.7.0
	6		Routine work. Evacuated 9 Horses & 3 Mules to No 4 V.E.S. - 1 Private Proceeded to Concentration Camp for dispersal - Capt W. Anderson assumed command of No 314 V.S. since Capt B. Winchey demobilized	2.7.0
	7		Section moved to BETTENHOVEN	
BETTENHOVEN	8		Routine work. 1 Horse LD from No 1 Section Light D.A.C. destroyed & sold for Butchery purposes	2.7.0
	9		Routine work	2.7.0
	10		Routine work	2.7.0

(A9175) Wt. W2358/P560 600,000 12/7 D. D. & L. Sch. 52a. Forms/C2118/15.

WAR DIARY
or
INTELLIGENCE SUMMARY.
(Erase heading not required.)

Army Form C. 2118.

No 3 M.V.S. Light Division

Place	Date	Hour	Summary of Events and Information	Remarks and references to Appendices
BETTENHOVEN	April 11		Routine work	8.7.0
	12		Routine work - 23 men proceeded to Concentration Camp for disposal	8.8.0
	13		Routine work - 2 men reported for duty with No. 3 M.V.S.	8.7.0
	14		Routine work - 1 man reported for duty with No. 3 M.V.S.	8.7.0
	15		Routine work	8.7.0
	16		Routine work - Evacuated 1 Horse & 1 Mule to No. 4 V.E.S.	8.7.0
	17		Routine work	8.7.0
	18		Section moved to HOLLENHOLZ FARM	
HOLLENHOLZ FARM	19		Routine work	8.7.0
	20		Routine work	8.7.0
	21		Routine work	8.7.0
	22		Routine work	8.7.0
	23		Routine work	8.7.0
	24		Routine work - Capt E.F. Nudler R.A.V.C. assumed command of No. 3 M.V.S. vice Capt J.W. Robinson	8.7.0
	25		Routine work	8.7.0

WAR DIARY
or
INTELLIGENCE SUMMARY.

Army Form C. 2118.

No 3 M.V.S. Light Division

Place	Date	Hour	Summary of Events and Information	Remarks and references to Appendices
HOLLENHOLZ FARM	April 26		Routine work	229
"	27		Routine work - Cpl Wilkin & Pte Cook Rowe proceed to England. Cmd'g for dispersal.	230
"	28		Routine work - Evacuated 4 horses to No 4 V.E.S	229
"	29		Routine work -	229
"	30		Routine work	229

E.S. Angler Capt Rave
O.C. No 3 M.V.S.
Light Division

3RD
MOBILE VETERINARY
SECT
No. ...
Date 5/5/19

WAR DIARY
or
INTELLIGENCE SUMMARY.
(Erase heading not required.)

Army Form C. 2118.

Place	Date	Hour	Summary of Events and Information	Remarks and references to Appendices
HOHENHOLZ FARM	May 1st		Routine work.	870
"	2nd		Routine work.	870
"	3rd		Routine work. Pte Searle reported to M.V.S. from Hospital	870
"	4th		Routine work.	870
"	5th		Routine work. Evacuated 1 Horse + 3 mules to ho. 4 V.E.S	870
"	6th		Routine work	877
"	7th		" "	877
"	8th		" "	877
"	9th		Routine work	877
"	10th		Routine work. 1 L.D. mule destroyed for Pathology purposes. H/Q 3rd Pl Pl. also 1 Rider from 3rd mne. reported to M.V.S. for Veterinary Course	3"
"	11th		Routine work. Sirs new reported to H.V.S. for Veterinary Course of 3 fm 20th A.R.R. 1st Indian Regt, 1 fr. R.P.C., 1 fr. 9 Pipr., 1 53rd Regt.	870
"	12th		Routine work	870
"	13th		Routine work	870
"	14th		Routine work 1 mule + 2 horses discharged fit to R.to to	870

Army Form C. 2118.

WAR DIARY
or
INTELLIGENCE SUMMARY.
(Erase heading not required.)

Place	Date	Hour	Summary of Events and Information	Remarks and references to Appendices
HOMENNEZ FARM	1 July		Routine work	
"	2		Notice board	
"	3rd		Routine work. Pte Lake shifted EOVS for transfer	
"	4th		Routine work	
"	5th		Routine work. Bar to Home + 3 men to 4 VES	
"	6th		Routine work	
"	7th		" " Boarded above 13 men + 4 ho to VES	
"	8th			
"	9th		Routine work	
"	10th		" "	
"	11th		Routine and " " distempers for stables of Marshall	
"	12th		2 tpts and one man goes to HVS for Veterinary course	
"	12th		2pl w ARR 1 Lcl 2 L + 1 pt ROH, 1 pt 3 pays + 1 stride	
"	13th		Routine work	
"	13th		" "	
"	14th		Routine work 1 h/s + 2 hors entrained to Rouen	

WAR DIARY
or
INTELLIGENCE SUMMARY.
(Erase heading not required.)

Army Form C. 2118.

Place	Date	Hour	Summary of Events and Information	Remarks and references to Appendices
HOHENHOLZ FARM	May 15		Routine work	370
"	16th		Routine work. 1 cart mule evacuated to No 4 V.E.S	370
"	17th		Routine work. 1 couple z'Bns. allotted from 2nd Arty Staffs	370
"	18th		Routine work	370
"	19th		Routine work. 1 van detailed to Rhine Army at D.H.Q. Pte Bradley W	370
			proceeded to U.K. on 14 days leave	370
"	20th		Routine work	370
"	21st		Routine work	370
"	22nd		Routine work	370
"	23rd		Routine work. Two horses & 1 mule evacuated to No 4 V.E.S	370
			a/Sergt Penver H. reported to MVS for duty	
"	24th		Routine work	370
"	25th		Routine work a/Sergt Smith proceeded on leave to U.K. from	370
			24/5/19 to 2/6/19	
"	26th		Routine work. The nine men on Veterinary Course returned to	370
			their units	

WAR DIARY
or
INTELLIGENCE SUMMARY.
(Erase heading not required.)

Army Form C. 2118.

Place	Date	Hour	Summary of Events and Information	Remarks and references to Appendices
ACHEAHOLZ FARM	June 15		Routine work	
"	16th		Routine work. Lectures & instructions to N.C.O.s, N.E.S.	
"	17th		Routine work. Inspection of M.T. by Lieut. L. A. Staff	
"	18th		Routine work	
"	19th		Routine work. Lecture & demonstration to Officers & N.C.O.s & D.W.R. Pte Priestley 4	
"	20th		proceeded to U.K. on 14 days leave	
"	21st		Routine work	
"	21st		Routine work	
"	22nd		Routine work	
"	23rd		Routine work. Four horses & mules dispatched to No 4 V.E.S.	
"	24th		Routine work. 2/Capt Green to report to M.V.S. for duty	
"	25th		Routine work. 2/Capt R.M. proceeded on leave to UK from 26/5/19 to 9/6/19	
"	26th		Routine work. Vet. care and Veterinary work attended to other units.	

WAR DIARY
or
INTELLIGENCE SUMMARY.
(Erase heading not required.)

Army Form C. 2118.

Place	Date	Hour	Summary of Events and Information	Remarks and references to Appendices
HOHENHOLZ FARM	May 27th		Routine work. Two Veterinary reported to M.V.S. for duty with a view to transfer to Rear.	2.7.0
"	28th		Routine work.	
"	29th		Routine work. Two L.D. Horses & 4 Risers evacuated to No. 4 V.E.S.	2.7.0
"	30th		Routine work. Three Rear Pers. reported for duty at M.V.S. from No. 24 Veterinary Hospital	2.7.0
"	31st		Routine work.	2.7.0

E A Anglin Capt Rane
O.C. No 3 M.V.S.
Light Division

6/6/19.

WAR DIARY
or
INTELLIGENCE SUMMARY.
(Erase heading not required.)

Army Form C. 2118.

Place	Date	Hour	Summary of Events and Information	Remarks and references to Appendices
ACHENHOLZ FARM	27th		Routine work. Two Veterinary reported to M.V.S. for duty with wires to transfer to Reserve	270
"	28th		Routine work.	
"	29th		Routine work. Five L.T. Horses & 4 Riders evacuated to no 6 V.E.S.	270
"	30th		Routine work. Three Race Hrs reported for duty at M.V.S. from no 24 Veterinary Hospital	270
"	31st		Routine work.	270

E.F. Ogilvie Capt R.A.V.C.
O.C. no 3 M.V.S.
Light Division

6/9/15

WAR DIARY or INTELLIGENCE SUMMARY.

(Erase heading not required.)

Army Form C. 2118.

No 3 MVS

Place	Date	Hour	Summary of Events and Information	Remarks and references to Appendices
HOHENHOLZ FARM	June 1st		Routine work in M.V.S.	E.J.Q.
"	2nd		Routine work – Sergt Hales W. Rowe sent to Concert Camp for demobilisation	E.J.Q.
"	3rd		Routine work in M.V.S.	E.J.Q.
"	4th		Routine work	E.J.Q.
"	5th		Routine work. Evacuated 4 Horses + 1 mule to No 4 V.E.S.	E.J.Q.
"	6th		Routine work. No. S.E. 20769 Pte Day V.H. Rowt admitted to Hospital	E.J.Q.
"	7th		Routine work	E.J.Q.
"	8th		Routine work	E.J.Q.
"	9th		Routine work – Sergt Smith Rowe returned from Base	E.J.Q.
"	10th		Routine work in M.V.S.	E.J.Q.
"	11th		Routine work - Evacuated 4 Horses + 1 mule to No 4 V.E.S. 77 0863 Pte Bradley W. Rowe returned from Base	E.J.Q.
"	12th		Routine work	E.J.Q.
"	13th		Routine work	E.J.Q.
"	14th		Routine work	E.J.Q.
"	15th		Routine work – 1 Sergt + 5 O.Rs sent to Remt Depot Cagne to collect H Remounts	E.J.Q.

Army Form C. 2118.

WAR DIARY
or
INTELLIGENCE SUMMARY.
(Erase heading not required.)

Instructions regarding War Diaries and Intelligence Summaries are contained in F.S. Regs., Part II. and the Staff Manual respectively. Title pages will be prepared in manuscript.

Place	Date	Hour	Summary of Events and Information	Remarks and references to Appendices
HOHENHOLZ FARM	June 16th		Routine work.	3.V.S.
"	17th		Routine work. - 4 Horses & 1 mule evacuated to No 4 V.E.S.	3.V.S.
"	18th		Routine work. - 1 Horse & 1 mule evacuated to No 4 V.E.S.	3.V.S.
"	19th		Routine work. - 1 Horse evacuated to No 4 V.E.S.	3.V.S.
"	20th		Routine work - Pte Day V.H. Rars reported for duty from 44 C.C.S.	3.V.S.
"	21st		Routine work	3.V.S.
"	22nd		Routine work	3.V.S.
"	23rd		Routine work - No 33595 Pte Best A. Rave reported for duty from No 10 M.V.S.	3.V.S.
"	24th		Routine work	3.V.S.
"	25th		Routine work to 3 M.V.S.	3.V.S.
"	26th		Routine work Capt Angler proceed to U.K. further steps from London June 29/6/19 to 11/7/19	3.V.S.
"	27th		Routine work No 770863 P.M. Brodly & 22 M.V.H. No. 2 and SE-23905 Pte Heflyn struck off strength of 3 M.V.S. & reputed with 24 Gen Hospital for entry.	3.V.S.
"	28th		Routine work to M.V.S.	3.V.S.
"	29th		Routine work to M.V.S.	3.V.S.
"	30th		Routine work	3.V.S.

E.A. Angler Capt R.a.v.c.
O.C. No 3 M.V.S.
Light Div.

D.A.D.V.S.
LIGHT DIVISION
Date 5/7 1919

3RD MOBILE VETERINARY SECTION.
Date 6/7/19

WAR DIARY
or
INTELLIGENCE SUMMARY.
(Erase heading not required.)

Army Form C. 2118.

Instructions regarding War Diaries and Intelligence Summaries are contained in F. S. Regs., Part II. and the Staff Manual respectively. Title pages will be prepared in manuscript.

Place	Date	Hour	Summary of Events and Information	Remarks and references to Appendices
CHYLES	13		Rations & work in M.V.S. Capt. R.J. Inglow Empl. Coma for Rome	
	14		Rations & work in M.V.S.	
	15		Rations & work in M.V.S.	
	16		Rations & work in M.V.S. Pte Van Rose returned to England	
	17		Rations & work in M.V.S.	
	18		Rations & work in M.V.S.	
	19		Rations & work in M.V.S.	
	20		Rations & work in M.V.S.	
	21		Rations & work in M.V.S.	
	22		Rations & work in M.V.S.	
	23		Rations & work in M.V.S.	
	24		Rations & work in M.V.S.	
	25		Rations & work in M.V.S.	
	26		Rations & work in M.V.S.	

WAR DIARY
or
INTELLIGENCE SUMMARY.

(Erase heading not required.)

Army Form C. 2118.

Place	Date	Hour	Summary of Events and Information	Remarks and references to Appendices
OHLIGS	27		Routine work in MVS	
	28		Routine work in MVS	
	29		Routine work in MVS. 44th Bgde Received Remounts from 38/9/15 & 39/9/15	
	30		Routine work in MVS	
	31		Routine work in MVS. Two horses evacuated to 2 V.E.S.	

E J Cowper Capt RAVC
O.C. No 3 M.V.S.

3RD
MOBILE VETERINARY
SECTION.

No 3 M.V.S.

Army Form C. 2118.

WAR DIARY
or
INTELLIGENCE SUMMARY.
(Erase heading not required.)

Place	Date	Hour	Summary of Events and Information	Remarks and references to Appendices
OHLIGS	August 1st		Routine work. 2 Horses evacuated to No 2 V.E.S.	2.7.9.
"	2nd		Routine work in M.V.S.	2.7.9.
"	3rd		Routine work in M.V.S.	2.7.9.
"	4th		Routine work in M.V.S. Ptes Jones & Webb 20th K.R.R. returned to their unit	2.7.9.
"	5th		Routine work in M.V.S.	2.7.9.
"	6th		Routine work in M.V.S.	2.7.9.
"	7th		Routine work in M.V.S. 1 Horse destroyed, visited by O. Colonel	2.7.9.
"	8th		Routine work in M.V.S.	2.7.9.
"	9th		Routine work in M.V.S.	2.7.9.
"	10th		Routine work in M.V.S. 17040 Pte Chivers Paus proceeded on Leave to U.K. from 11/8/19 to 25/8/19.	2.7.9.
"	11th		Routine work in M.V.S.	2.7.9.
"	12th		Routine work in M.V.S. 2 Horses evacuated to No 2 V.E.S.	2.7.9.
"	13th		Routine work in M.V.S.	2.7.9.
"	14th		Routine work in M.V.S.	2.7.9.
"	15th		Routine work in M.V.S. S/Sgt Bay Paus returned from leave U.K. Pte Humphries Paus proceeded on leave to U.K. from 16/8/19 to 30/8/19	2.7.9.

WAR DIARY
or
INTELLIGENCE SUMMARY.
(Erase heading not required.)

Army Form C. 2118.

Place	Date	Hour	Summary of Events and Information	Remarks and references to Appendices
OHLIGS	16th		Routine work in M.V.S.	272.
"	17th		Routine work in M.V.S. Prazer Rose proceeded on leave to U.K.	272.
			from 15/8/19 to 1/9/19	
"	18th		Routine work in M.V.S. 5'5" Horses transferred to Cologne from Bringhurst	272.
"	19th		Routine work in M.V.S.	272.
"	20th		Routine work in M.V.S. The Colonel R.A.S.C. inspected our horses &	272.
			U.K. from 21/8/19 to 4/9/19	
"	21st		Routine work in M.V.S. 1 Horse & 3 mules destroyed, sent to Potters	272.
"	22nd		Routine work in M.V.S. Q6 M.& Bg Rose proceeded on leave to U.K.	272.
			A.D.V.S. Visited the two tractor stables from 23/8/19 to 6/9/19	
"	23rd		Routine work in M.V.S. — Major B. Barr & C.C. Reid Rose inspected Barns	272.
"	24th		Routine work in M.V.S.	272.
"	25th		Routine work in M.V.S.	272.
"	26th		Routine work in M.V.S. Pte. Owens Rose returned from leave to U.K.	272.
"	27th		Routine work in M.V.S.	272.
"	28th		Routine work in M.V.S.	272.

Army Form C. 2118.

WAR DIARY
or
INTELLIGENCE SUMMARY.
(Erase heading not required.)

Place	Date	Hour	Summary of Events and Information	Remarks and references to Appendices
OHLIGS	August 29th		Routine work in M.V.S. 13 Horses + 5 Mules Evacuated to No 2 V.E.S.	270
"	30th		1 Horse + 1 mule destroyed value to Butcher 2720 fcs. Picture work in M.V.S. Pte Oliver Rous invested & inoculated. Cant. Clispie for privileges.	270
"	31st		Routine work in M.V.S	270

F.J. Angler Capt. R.A.V.C.
O.C. No 3 Mobile Vety Section
27th Divn

3RD
MOBILE VETERINARY
SECT
Date 6/9/19

WAR DIARY
or
INTELLIGENCE SUMMARY.
(Erase heading not required.)

Army Form C. 2118.

Place	Date	Hour	Summary of Events and Information	Remarks and references to Appendices
OH/GS	Sept.n 1st		Routine work in MVS. 2 Horses destroyed one sent to Bailey College	272
"	2		ADVS & Capt. inspected the Sect.	272
"	3		Routine work in H.V.S.	272
"	4		Pte 20660 Pte Nelson transferred Brit. U.K. (gun) to 6 M.F.S. (14 days) two horses evacuated to 6 M.F.S.	272
"	5		Routine work in MVS.	272
"	6		Pte 2112 M.V.S. D. Reilly R.V.C. returned to duty	272
"	7		Routine work in MVS.	272
"	8		Routine work in MVS. Pte Hartley + Pte Humphries returned from leave. Pte Humphries granted 7 days between Lucks + days in M.V.S. S.E. 2708 Pte Humphreys (water supply) evacuated for paralysis	272
"	9		Routine work in MVS.	272
"	10		Routine work in MVS. 12 Horses + 3 mules evacuated to 2 V.E.S.	272
"	11		Routine work in MVS.	
"	12		Routine work in H.V.S.	

WAR DIARY or INTELLIGENCE SUMMARY

Army Form C. 2118.

Place	Date	Hour	Summary of Events and Information	Remarks and references to Appendices
O.H. & G.S.	Sept 13		Routine work in M.V.S. 4 mules evacuated to No 2 V.E.S	772
"	14		Routine work in M.V.S.	772
"	15		Routine work in M.V.S. ADVS VI Corps inspected Section	772
"	16		Routine work 1 Horse destroyed - sent to Butcher Shop	772
"	17		Routine work in M.V.S.	772
"	18		Routine work in M.V.S. 1 Horse destroyed + sent to Butcher Shop	772
"	19		Routine work in M.V.S. 6 Horses + 1 Mule evacuated to No 2 V.E.S	772
"	20		Routine work in M.V.S.	772
"	21		Routine work in M.V.S.	772
"	22		Routine work in M.V.S.	772
"	23		Routine work in M.V.S. OC Callow + tempte Rose sent to enumerate camp Cheps for numbers	772
"	24		Routine work in M.V.S. Temp Infantry Regs reported our evacuation to No 2 V.E.S. 3 Horses sent to Boulogne Depot + one alumentatus	772
"	25		Routine work in M.V.S. Nine horses sent to Divil Collecting Camp	772
"	26		Routine work in M.V.S.	772

Army Form C. 2118.

WAR DIARY
or
INTELLIGENCE SUMMARY.
(Erase heading not required.)

Instructions regarding War Diaries and Intelligence Summaries are contained in F. S. Regs., Part II. and the Staff Manual respectively. Title pages will be prepared in manuscript.

Place	Date	Hour	Summary of Events and Information	Remarks and references to Appendices
OHLIOS	Oct 27		Routine work in M.V.S	870
	28		Routine work in M.V.S	870
	29		Routine work in M.V.S	870
	30		Routine work in M.V.S	870

H. Ongles Capt. R.A.V.C.
O.C. No 3 M.V.S
Legh Division

6/11/15

Army Form C. 2118.

WAR DIARY
or
INTELLIGENCE SUMMARY.
(Erase heading not required.)

Place	Date	Hour	Summary of Events and Information	Remarks and references to Appendices
OHLIGS	October 1st		Routine work in M.V.S.	370
"	2nd		Routine work in M.V.S. 9 Horse evacuated to No 1 V.E.S. & 1 Horse sent to Remount Depot	370
"	3		Routine work in M.V.S.	370
"	4		Routine work in M.V.S.	370
"	5		Routine work in M.V.S.	370
"	6		Routine work in M.V.S.	370
"	7		Routine work in M.V.S.	370
"	8		Routine work in M.V.S.	370
"	9		Routine work in M.V.S. Six horses & 1 mule evacuated to No 1 V.E.S.	370
"	10		Routine work in M.V.S.	370
"	11		Routine work in M.V.S.	370
"	12		Routine work in M.V.S.	370
"	13		Routine work in M.V.S. O/C Vet. Post proceeded on leave to U.K.	370
"	14		Routine work in M.V.S.	370
"	15		Routine work in M.V.S.	370

WAR DIARY
or
INTELLIGENCE SUMMARY.

(Erase heading not required.)

Army Form C. 2118.

Place	Date	Hour	Summary of Events and Information	Remarks and references to Appendices
OHLIGS	October 16		Routine work in M.V.S. Two horses evacuated to No 2 V.E.S.	370
"	17		Routine work in M.V.S. 7 Horses + 3 mules evac. to No 2 V.E.S. 1 mule sent to Remounts	370
"	18		Routine work in M.V.S.	370
"	19		Routine work in M.V.S.	370
"	20		Routine work in M.V.S. P/Sgt Glover Power proceeded to Quarantine camp for demobilization. 11 Ambulances attached to M.V.S. returned to their units. Surg Shoe Sh + S/Sh Wright + 2 Drs R.A.S.C. transferred to No 1 Cav Light Divn 2 Sanm - also 1 Horse Ambulance + G.S. wagon handed over to No 1 Cy Divn.	370
"	27		Part of equipment of No 3 M.V.S. returned to Ordnance.	370
"	28		Remainder of equipment of No 3 M.V.S. returned to Ordnance.	370

E.F. Ongley Capt. R.A.V.C.
O.C. No 3 M.V.S.
Light Divn

www.ingramcontent.com/pod-product-compliance
Lightning Source LLC
Chambersburg PA
CBHW080911230426
43667CB00015B/2650